T0316466

THE ECONOMICS
OF SMALL HOLDINGS

THE ECONOMICS
OF SMALL HOLDINGS

A STUDY BASED ON A SURVEY
OF SMALL SCALE FARMING
IN CARMARTHENSHIRE

by

EDGAR THOMAS

Agricultural Economics Research Institute
University of Oxford

WITH PREFACE BY
C. S. ORWIN

CAMBRIDGE
AT THE UNIVERSITY PRESS
1927

CAMBRIDGE
UNIVERSITY PRESS

University Printing House, Cambridge CB2 8BS, United Kingdom

Cambridge University Press is part of the University of Cambridge.

It furthers the University's mission by disseminating knowledge in the pursuit of education, learning and research at the highest international levels of excellence.

www.cambridge.org
Information on this title: www.cambridge.org/9781107586727

© Cambridge University Press 1927

First published 1927
First paperback edition 2015

A catalogue record for this publication is available from the British Library

ISBN 978-1-107-58672-7 Paperback

PREFACE

IN the multitude of proposals for the better organisation of rural Britain there is none which has received more general assent than that which is directed towards the closer settlement of the land. The older political parties of the State have this plank common to their platforms; many serious students of rural reform are advocates of the multiplication of small holdings; whilst the town dweller, if ever he thinks of agricultural problems, has generally the re-creation of the "peasant" in his mind. In these circumstances it is the more surprising that action has preceded investigation, and that whilst much has been attempted by the legislature in this direction, still more is demanded of it notwithstanding that evidence upon the relative economic and social values of holdings of different sizes is almost entirely lacking. This is not to say that the subject has not engaged the attention of agricultural students. On the contrary, a voluminous literature upon it exists, but very little has been based upon statistical investigation. 'Damnable iteration' takes the place of evidence, and that which anybody may assert is assumed to be true.

It is probable that the demand for the subdivision of farms in this country arises—apart from purely political considerations—from the prevalence of small-scale farming in extensive areas of continental Europe. Travellers see the family farmer at work everywhere upon his small holding. They note his obvious industry, his seeming content and the high standard of cultivation to which so frequently he attains. From this they argue that the re-population of the English countryside, and the increased productivity of its broad acres, can be achieved at one stroke by the subdivision of the larger holdings which are a prominent feature of its farming systems. They do not stop to observe the long hours of labour involved in peasant farming, the heavy toll on the family from which not even the smallest toddler is exempt, nor the low standard of living with which their work may be so often rewarded. They do not realise the complete absence, in many cases, of alternative forms of employment, which, on the other hand, are so abundant in our own country with its highly developed industrial system and its almost boundless colonial empire. Nor do they study economic history to the point of learning that England began more than a hundred years ago to emerge from a condition of things similar to that which excites their admiration abroad, and that the evolution of her larger units of production cannot be regarded as a retrograde movement without more careful investigation.

These observations must not be construed as a prejudgment of the small holdings question in the opposite sense. They are put forward only to show the need for more thorough study of the subject with a view to the determination of the economic unit of cultivation under various conditions, and the organisation of the tenure of land best calculated to secure the social well-being of those engaged in agricultural industry. The fact is that very little research directed to these ends has been undertaken. The most important study of the general problem made in this country is that carried out by Mr A. W. Ashby in the years 1913 and 1914 and published in 1917, though, owing to a title which conveys the impression of a merely local application, his work has not received that degree of publicity to which it is entitled[1]. Prior to this, the economics of large and small holdings in England had been investigated by a German economist, Dr Hermann Levy, of the University of Heidelberg. The English version of his study was published in 1911 and attracted a good deal of attention[2]. His conclusions are drawn mainly from observation, statistical data being almost entirely absent, and while his reasoning brings him often to a sound conclusion as, for example, when he indicates the superiority of the large unit for most purposes of arable farming, his deductions in many important matters are entirely fallacious. Some of his errors are due to a lack of knowledge of local agricultural history, as when he assumes that the large farms created after the inclosure of Exmoor Forest were the result of engrossment, the facts being that they were evolved by an enthusiastic land reclaimer, at enormous cost to himself, out of the wild to which they speedily returned[3]. Others, and these are more serious, are merely mis-statements, as when Dr Levy asserts that the farmer "has to be constantly on the watch" lest the labourer's dislike of milking should find expression "in some careless or unkind handling of the beasts," which he contrasts with "the loving attention" of the smallholder[4]; or when he asserts that after decreasing in number for a century or more small homesteads are again on the increase[5], and that English landlords, "after a century of contrary practice, endeavour to divide their farms and to reduce them to the size which was the rule in the England of the past."[6]

---

[1] A. W. Ashby, *Allotments and Small Holdings in Oxfordshire*, pp. vi + 198 (Oxford University Press), 5s. This work consists of a survey of the general problem illustrated by reference to examples from the county named.

[2] Hermann Levy, *Large and Small Holdings*, translated by Ruth Kenyon, pp. viii + 249 (Cambridge University Press).

[3] *Op. cit.* p. 50.   [4] *Op. cit.* p. 173.   [5] *Op. cit.* p. 182.

[6] *Op. cit.* p. 203.

But most serious of all are the mistakes which occur owing to his failure to appreciate the implications of his own observations and conclusions:—

They (i.e. hired workers) want to have their Sundays free for enjoyment and for their best clothes, and not to be obliged to be at the cow-sheds at certain hours to milk or feed the cows[1].

A dairy farmer producing on a large scale...has very important disadvantages as compared with a small farmer who does the work himself with the aid of his family and employs little or no outside labour[2].

The first question in regard to poultry-keeping is whether the wife of the occupier is prepared to take part in the work of the farm, not merely with her head, but with her hands.... Poultry will only pay where the farmer's wife and daughters will themselves look after them[3].

These are but a few examples of statements leading only to one possible conclusion—of which Dr Levy gives no indication—namely that, in the cases cited, the apparent advantage of the small farmer is achieved only at the cost of his standard of living.

There is no disparagement of Dr Levy's work intended by these criticisms, which are made merely to indicate once more the need for more accurate data upon which to form opinions and by which to formulate agricultural policy. The account of the investigations of Mr Edgar Thomas, contained in the following pages, is a contribution to this need. Himself a member of a farming family, he has taken a district containing a high proportion of small farms, with which he has a life-long acquaintance, for the purpose of an intensive study of the economic position of the small cultivator, particularly in contrast with that of the wage-labourer. Never before has any

---

[1] *Op. cit.* p. 173. [2] *Op. cit.* p. 177. [3] *Op. cit.* pp. 178–9.

attempt been made to compare the financial position of
the two by taking account of the market value of his own
long hours of work and of the unpaid labour given to the
family-farmer by his wife and children, and the results
deserve the closest consideration. That the financial test
is not the only one, not, possibly, even the most important
one, must not be overlooked, but in a country where so
much alternative employment is available to the youth
of both sexes it becomes a serious consideration whether
work under the conditions disclosed can compete with that
which is remunerated with a larger shilling, and whether
more discrimination may not be needed between the types
of farming most suited to development in small units.

Mr Thomas' study was made, primarily, for the purpose
of the research degree of B.Litt.; it was extended to the
consideration of certain conditions of small cultivation
in some continental countries, the results of which are
contained in Appendix C to this volume.

C. S. ORWIN

Agricultural Economics Research Institute
Oxford

December 1926

CONTENTS

SECTION I

INTRODUCTION

1. PRELIMINARY STATEMENT

So much has been written on the economics of large and small holdings that a justification should be demanded for the appearance of yet another study on the subject, since, so far as its general treatment is concerned, it is probably impossible to write anything new. However, most of the literature on the problem has been, in this country at least, almost entirely lacking in extensive and reliable data illustrating how the smallholder lives. The sole aim of this study is to attempt to remedy this deficiency by presenting the results of both an extensive and an intensive survey of a community of smallholders, thereby revealing something of their true economic position.

Inasmuch as there is a veritable library available on the various social, economic, and technical aspects of the question of the size of the agricultural unit, it is only necessary, here, to give a very brief summary of the main arguments that have been adduced, from time to time, for and against the small holding[1].

2. DEFINITION OF UNIT

In the first place it is necessary to define the unit employed, and for this purpose it is useful to regard the holding, first, as a source of income, and, secondly, as a field of activity for its occupier[2]. On this basis the lower

[1] For convenience, special reference may be made to (1) *Large and Small Holdings* (Cambridge University Press), by Hermann Levy, chapters VII and IX; (2) *Allotments and Small Holdings in Oxfordshire* (Oxford University Press), by A. W. Ashby, part II, chapters I and VII, where the various arguments mentioned here are developed.

[2] Levy, *op. cit.* p. 88.

limit of size for the small holding must be that which will just keep its occupier fully employed, and will just provide him with the wherewithall for the sustenance of himself and his family. It is much more difficult to fix the upper limit for the small holding, because the line of demarcation between it and the medium-sized farm is by no means clearly drawn. For the purpose of legislation this upper limit has been fixed at 50 acres or £50 rent. The introduction of the two tests—acreage and rent—compensates for the shortcomings of either used alone. For example, a holding of 100 acres of indifferent land might represent all the characteristics of a small holding, but by the acreage test alone it would be included with the large farms. Again, another holding of only 25 acres of excellent land might be rented at £55; thus, by the rent test alone, it would be barred from its obvious inclusion amongst small holdings. By means of this double test an attempt is made to convert all types of land into terms of a common unit, the unit adopted being an acre of land valued at £1 an acre. Using this basis, the upper limit of size for small holdings will be that holding containing land equivalent to fifty such units. A more satisfactory method, however, is to differentiate between the small holding and the medium farm on the basis of the degree of separation of managerial and manual labour, and on the degree of capitalisation obtaining. Generally speaking, the medium-sized farm differs from the small holding in that, first, the occupier needs to employ wage labour, and, secondly, there is a certain division between manual labour and the work of organisation. It will be seen, then, that every case has to be examined separately, since it is not so much the size of the holding as the nature of its organisation which will determine whether it be a small holding or not.

3. ARGUMENTS FOR SMALL HOLDINGS

"From the point of view of the national balance of the population, and from the standpoint of general social economics, the case for small holdings has received a wide provisional acceptance."[1] The main arguments that have secured this are briefly as follows. In the first place, small holdings support a large number of persons per acre, and thereby act as a palliative for rural depopulation, while they remedy the very common defect of the underfarming of land by farmers who attempt to cultivate too large an area. Again, by necessitating a more intensive system of cultivation, they result in greater production per acre. The defects from which they are supposed to suffer in their limited access to capital or credit, and marketing facilities, can be compensated by the development of co-operation. It is thus argued that in this way they are able to achieve the same results as large-scale production without the attendant hardships which this form of production has so often brought to the worker in industry. They are also calculated to foster certain socially desirable characteristics such as thrift, sobriety, and diligence; they are of value to those people who are not in love with working to orders, and they form the first rung in the so-called "agricultural" or "rural" social ladder. Lastly, they possess an important political significance inasmuch as they distribute property or its control, thereby acting as a bulwark against revolutionary change.

[1] "Some Considerations Relating to the Position of the Small Holding in the United Kingdom," by Prof. W. G. S. Adams, M.A., *Journal of the Royal Statistical Society*, Sept. 1907.

4. ARGUMENTS AGAINST SMALL HOLDINGS

Each of the foregoing merits has been contradicted by the protagonists of the large farm, who claim that the industrialised agricultural enterprise is a more economically sound palliative for rural unrest. Thus, small holdings are said to be wasteful of land, necessitating the withdrawal from productive use of large areas in the form of boundaries, etc., while the crucial test is not so much maximum production per acre as maximum production per person employed. Secondly, they are equally uneconomic units for the use of capital, necessitating a large initial outlay, on buildings, etc., of money which would otherwise be available for more productive purposes. Thirdly, they do not provide scope for division of labour or for the specialisation of capacity and skill. These three defects make them a stumbling-block to all scientific progress, since it is maintained that "in every branch of human enterprise maximum production at low cost in labour or in capital has been synonymous with large scale organisation."[1] Again, the supposed "independence of the smallholder is often purchased dearly at the cost of the excessive labour of the occupier and the sweating of his family."[2] Further, the small holding is not the best school for the prospective manager of the large farm, since often the ascent of the social ladder is dependent on the "cautiousness and frugality of the smallholder, and the effect of his life experience is to make him a very conservative farmer."[3] Lastly, successful small holdings are practically confined to *petite culture*; therefore, the market for their products is strictly limited, and small holdings cannot be extended indefinitely.

[1] "The Small Holdings Craze," by C. S. Orwin, M.A., *Edinburgh Review*, April 1916.
[2] *Agriculture after the War*, by Sir A. D. Hall, p. 54. [3] Ashby, *op. cit.* p. 99.

5. TENTATIVE CONCLUSIONS

It will be seen from this brief *résumé* that the problem of the unit of production in agriculture is, really, an epitome of the wider economic problem of large *versus* small scale production, and, like it, allows no finality of treatment. Assuming, then, that the various size units have their place in the agricultural economy of every country, it remains to try to establish some connection between the respective economic advantages of large and small holdings in relation to the various branches of farming[1]. And it is possible to establish roughly the following three-fold classification. First come those branches of farming, such as corn growing and sheep farming, which are pre-eminently suited for large-scale production; here success is dependent on the free use of capital in the form of land or of labour-saving machinery. The second group contains those branches requiring comparatively small outlay of capital, in which success depends to a larger extent upon that "qualitative intensity of work which is the prerogative of the smallholder with his personal and family labour"[2]—such are pig keeping and poultry rearing, which are pre-eminently suited for the small holding. The third group is by far the largest and contains such branches of farming as cattle rearing, dairying, vegetable and fruit growing. All of these are suited under differing circumstances to both large and small scale farming, since, sometimes, possession of capital and the use of machinery will compensate for the absence of personal supervision; while, *vice versa*, under other circumstances the qualitative intensity of the small farmer's work will make up for the lack of the various advantages of large-scale production.

[1] Levy, *op. cit.* pp. 156–183; also Ashby, *op. cit.* pp. 172–179.
[2] Levy, *op. cit.* p. 166.

6. OUTLINE OF STUDY

It is now possible to outline the scope of the present investigation which divides itself into three sections. In the second section, which is descriptive of the area investigated, a fairly comprehensive census is attempted of a community of smallholders. The main contribution of the study is given in the third section, which presents the results of an extensive survey of the general economic conditions of this community of smallholders, followed by a more intensive study of their true economic position. An appendix has been added as a possible source of comparison which contains summaries of similar studies in four European countries where work of this nature has long been placed on a systematic and scientific footing.

SECTION II

GENERAL AND HISTORICAL OUTLINE OF THE AREA OF THE STUDY

1. THE COUNTY OF CARMARTHEN

The unit taken for the present survey is the administrative County of Carmarthen, which is the largest of the Welsh counties and is 587,816 acres in extent.

The surface of the county conforms for the greater part to a tableland running east and west between the two rivers Teifi and Tywi. This tableland is intersected by numerous streamlets running into the larger rivers, which make the county a succession of hill and dale. For the greater part the hills do not attain any considerable height, and the hillsides are capable of arable cultivation, although they are generally used for grazing purposes. The northern part of the county is more mountainous, the Black Mountains on the Breconshire borders attaining to an elevation of over 2500 feet. The climate of this northern part is, therefore, somewhat colder than that of the south which lies nearer the sea. Exposure to the south-west anti-trade winds and the presence of the mountains are together responsible for the high rainfall, which varies from 40 inches per annum in the south to 45 inches per annum in the north of the county.

The chief geological formations belong to the Ordovician and Silurian systems, and consist for the greater part of shales and sandstone. The Old Red Sandstone is the principal formation south of the Tywi, followed by the Carboniferous Limestone and Millstone Grit. The south-eastern region of the county contains important coal measures and forms part of the South Wales anthracite coalfield. The best agricultural land in the county is associated with the three largest rivers—the Tywi, the Taf, and the Teifi—the valley of the Tywi is one of the most fertile districts in Wales.

2. GENERAL CHARACTER OF CARMARTHENSHIRE FARMING

The systems of farming vary with the configuration of the county, and three main types can be roughly distinguished. At the one extreme is the sheep farming of the Breconshire hinterland, and at the other the dairy holdings of the valleys, while in between is the predominant system of mixed husbandry depending a little on every variety of produce. It might be said that the chief aim of Carmarthenshire farmers is the production of milk, butter, and meat for the ready market which lies so close at hand in the neighbouring densely populated industrial centres.

The production of milk for sale is confined to the valleys of the Tywi and the Taf. Much of this milk finds a ready market in the immediate industrial areas, some goes so far afield as London, while important butter factories at Whitland and St Clears absorb a great deal of the milk of the surrounding districts. An attempt to establish a co-operative milk depot at Carmarthen has, so far, met with unfortunate results. In the more extensive and remote regions of the county the conversion of milk into butter is still a domestic process on the farms. This butter finds a primary market in the local market towns of which Carmarthen and Llandeilo are the most important. Practically all the meat is disposed of in the weekly marts which are firmly established at all the important centres in the county, although some trade is also transacted at the few fairs that still survive. Both fat stock and store cattle are sold. Sheep are also reared in considerable quantities, and the county carries a larger complement of pigs and horses than any other in Wales. There is also a considerable production of poultry and eggs. The details of the crops and stock in the county are given in the following table, which shows, in a summarised form, the official statistics of the agriculture of the county.

TABLE I. Acreage under crops and grass; and number of live stock on June 4th, 1923[1]

	Acres
Total acreage under crops and grass	413,134
Permanent grass for hay	93,922
Permanent grass not for hay	251,852
Rough grazings	93,318

Arable land:

	Acres
Oats	19,812
Barley	6,301
Mixed corn	5,496
Wheat	3,787
Clover and rotation grasses	22,196
Potatoes	2,953
Turnips and swedes	3,235
Mangolds	1,099
Other crops	1,600
Bare fallow	899

Number of horses	22,338
„ cattle	117,834
„ sheep	258,116
„ pigs	31,781

The essentially pastoral nature of the farming is well illustrated in this table, which shows that only 16 per cent. of the total cultivated area is returned as arable land. The cold, wet, and cloudy weather accounts for the fact that oats, barley, and a mixture of these two, are the grain crops most extensively grown. Oats make up 30 per cent. of the total arable area, while wheat takes fourth place,

---

[1] *Agricultural Statistics*, 1923, vol. LVIII, part I, Table II.

larger areas of both barley and mixed corn being grown. Only 12 per cent. of the total arable area is devoted to green crops—turnips, swedes, and mangolds; and a further 2 per cent. is under potatoes. The area under clover and rotation grasses is relatively large, accounting for nearly 33 per cent. of the total arable area. Carmarthenshire is not particularly suited for fruit culture, and the total area of orchards is returned as only 188 acres.

3. POPULATION

Although Carmarthen is one of the most important agricultural counties in Wales, yet, judged from the statistics of its population, agriculture is relatively un-important in the county itself. This is entirely due to the dense concentration of population within less than 20 per cent. of its total area which occurs in the eastern part of the county. Not only does this region form a part of the South Wales anthracite area, but some important metallurgical industries are also situated here. Thus, in 1921, of the county's total occupied adult population only 14,446 or less than 20 per cent. were returned as engaged in farming[1]. In spite of this, however, it is safe to state that the greater part of the county is still essentially agricultural in occupation, and the mental outlook of its people is equally essentially rural.

By emphasising its predominantly peasant nature, an analysis of the agricultural population of the county supplies a cogent reason for its selection as the field for the present study. Table II, which is abridged from the census report of 1921, gives the numbers of males and females of 12 years of age and upwards engaged in agricultural occupations in the county.

[1] 1921 *Census Report on the County of Carmarthen*, Table XVI.

TABLE II. Persons, 12 years of age and over, engaged in agriculture in Carmarthenshire in 1921[1]

	Males	Females	Total	%
Farmers	5,087	842	5,929	41·0
Relatives	2,142	807	2,949	20·5
Bailiffs and foremen ...	65	3	68	0·5
Shepherds	10	0	10	0·1
Cattlemen	283	480	763	5·3
Horsemen	616	2	618	4·3
Ordinary labourers ...	2,851	707	3,558	24·6
	3,825	1,192	5,017	34·8
Foresters and woodmen	114	0	114	0·8
Nurserymen, gardeners, seedsmen, etc. ...	348	10	358	2·4
Others	71	8	79	0·5
Total	11,587	2,859	14,446	100·0

It will be seen that the total number of hired persons (males and females) employed on Carmarthenshire farms is only 5017. According to the agricultural returns for the same year, there were 8766 agricultural holdings in the county, and of these 3114 were returned as being over 50 acres in extent[2]. Even allowing for a large number of small holdings in the occupation of persons classified under non-agricultural headings for census purposes, it is sufficiently clear from these figures that a large number of farms in the county employ no hired labour at all. In other words, it would seem from these figures that a majority of the farms in the county must be "family farms," where the entire work is done by the occupier and his family[3]. Thus, while farmers and their relatives

[1] 1921 *Census Report on the County of Carmarthen*, Table XVI.
[2] *Agricultural Statistics* 1921, part I, Table II.
[3] A similar argument illustrating the domestic nature of (1) Welsh farms in general is given in the *Welsh Land Report*, 1896, p. 148; (2) Carmarthen-

make up 61·5 per cent. of all persons employed in agriculture in Carmarthenshire, the corresponding number for the whole of England and Wales is only about 28 per cent.[1]

4. HISTORICAL SKETCH OF SMALL HOLDINGS IN CARMARTHENSHIRE

The history of the size of holdings in Wales is intimately related to the tribal organisation of Welsh society. It is not possible or necessary here to examine the interrelation of these factors; it is sufficient to state that "from time immemorial the holdings in Wales have generally been of small extent, inasmuch as the system of gavel-kind, which was the rule of inheritance in the country, resulted in the subdivision of holdings no less than estates."[2] The process by which these early tribal conditions have developed into the modern state of affairs is also beyond the scope of this work.

For the modern period of agricultural history, however, evidence of movements in the size of holdings in the country is fuller and less controversial, making it possible to follow the main changes that have occurred.

shire farms in particular, in *Wages and Conditions of Employment in Agriculture*, Cmd. 25, 1919, vol. II, p. 423.

On p. xxiv of the *Census Report on the County* (1921) the ratio of agricultural labourers (males) per 100 farmers and relatives is given as 39 for all the rural districts of the county, and the following comment is made: "The ratio of labourers to farmers supplies some information as to the character of the operations carried on; it tends to be high where farms are large and tillage prevails, and low in upland and grazing farms and in the districts where allotments and small holdings are numerous. The values of this ratio in the rural districts of Carmarthenshire contrast very sharply with those found in some of the eastern counties of England; e.g. the ratio is 449 for the aggregate of the rural districts of West Suffolk. In Glamorgan the corresponding ratio is 70, in Breconshire 56, in Cardiganshire 54, and in Pembrokeshire 63."

[1] *Census of England and Wales*, 1921, Table I, pp. 2, 3.

[2] *Report of the Royal Commission on Land in Wales and Monmouthshire*, C. 8221, 1896, p. 328.

If the existence of well-kept hedges may be taken as signifying a fairly extensive state of division of holdings, Carmarthenshire was, early in the eighteenth century, ahead of the rest of Wales in this respect, since in a rhyming account of the Welsh counties, written about the year 1720, the farmers of the county are awarded premier place on account of their well-kept fences[1]. Definite evidence as to the average size of holdings towards the close of the eighteenth century is given in the report on the farming of the county by Charles Hassal who stated that

in several parts of the district there are farms of considerable extent to be met with; some of three, four, or five hundred acres; but the great mass of county inclosed and tenanted, consists of very small farms of from one hundred acres down to thirty; and perhaps fifty or sixty acres may be taken as the average of a very large majority of the farms in the county of Carmarthen[2].

This was generally corroborated by Walter Davies, who wrote the account of South Wales in the second series of agricultural surveys published by the old Board of Agriculture in 1815[3].

Although no direct statistical evidence exists as to the

---

[1] Thus D. T. in *Hanes Tair Sir ar Ddeg Cymru*:

"Gwrychoedd union gwedi eu plannu
Am hyn yw'r hwsmyn goreu Ynghymru."

[2] *General View of the Agriculture of the County of Carmarthen*, by C. Hassal, p. 11.

[3] *General View of the Domestic Economy of South Wales*, by Walter Davies, p. 162: "In respect of the size of farms, one county seems to be only a counterpart of the other—we heard of but two gentlemen who occupied upwards of 1400 acres each, one in Cardiganshire and the other in Pembrokeshire.—Next to farms of the above extraordinary size, there are few from 800 to 600 acres; from 500 to 300 they become numerous; and from 200 to 100 acres still more so. The general run of the smaller farms is about 30 to 100 acres and the average of the whole district may be between 50 and 60 acres."

fortunes of small holdings between 1815 and 1875, nevertheless, the existence of a general tendency for consolidation of farms has been fairly well established as characteristic of the period. Direct evidence of its existence in
Wales is limited to the protests against the process which
appeared from time to time in contemporary Welsh
periodicals[1], while the Commissioners who reported in
1843 on the "Rebecca Riots" in South Wales mentioned
the consolidation of holdings as one of the agrarian causes
responsible for the incendiarism which then occurred in
Carmarthenshire and Pembrokeshire[2].

From 1875 onwards statistical evidence of the fortunes
of small holdings exists. An official estimate for that year
shows that, of all the holdings accounted for in the county,
84 per cent. were under 100 acres in extent, and 74 per
cent. of these were under 50 acres[3]. The numbers of
holdings under 5 acres are not given separately, but by
1885 the 1 to 5 acre group contained 13·1 per cent. of all
holdings. The chief changes that have occurred from 1885
onwards are illustrated in Table III, which gives the
periodic official figures of the numbers of small holdings
in the county.

During the decade from 1885 to 1895 a decrease of 169
is registered in the number of holdings in the 1 to 5 acre
group. Meanwhile there was an increase in the number of
both the 5 to 20 acre group and the 20 to 50 acre group.
In a county like Carmarthen, with an increasing urban
area within its bounds, allowance must be made for certain
developments which may have no reflex in the official
statistics. In the first place, many of the holdings in the

---

[1] (1) *Y Diwygiwr*, August 1840, p. 239; (2) *Llythyrau'r Hen Ffarmwr*, by
Dr W. Rees (1849), pp. 52–54, Letter XIX; (3) *Y Faner*, Articles by Thomas
Gee, 1857.
[2] C. 8221, *op. cit.* p. 326.   [3] C. 1303 (1875).

TABLE III. Numbers of small holdings in Carmarthenshire since 1885

Size of holding (acres)	1885*	1895†	1905‡	1912§	1917‖	1921¶	1923**
1–5	1106	937	1038	1044	976	909	867
5–20	2137	2340	} 4520	4584 {	2373	2487	2369
20–50	1852	1918			2114	2256	2203
Total: 1–50	5095	5195	5558	5628	5463	5652	5439

* C. 4848.   † C. 8502.   ‡ Cd. 3061.   § Cd. 6597.   ‖ Cd. 9006.
¶ *Agric. Statistics*, 1921, vol. LVI, part I.
** *Agric. Statistics*, 1923, vol. LVIII, part I.

immediate vicinity of the growing towns have, undoubtedly, been absorbed by the spread of such areas. But of far greater importance in Carmarthenshire has been the appearance of a new type of smallholder in the person of the coalminer, who supplements his industrial earnings by his occupation of a small holding. It will be shown later that the number of such "industrial smallholders" is considerable in the county. Allowance must, therefore, be made for the possibility of the increase in the number of small holdings thus brought about to neutralise any decrease resulting from consolidation of farms which may have occurred simultaneously in the rural areas. That such a process of consolidation was in progress at this period is amply proved by the evidence tendered to the Royal Commission on Land in Wales and Monmouthshire which reported in 1896 in the following terms:

We have reserved to the last the County of Carmarthen, which furnishes us with the most numerous complaints against consolidation, as it also seemed to us to be the county most under the domination of land hunger. There was scarcely a parish in its northern portion for which we were not furnished with exhaustive lists, giving the names of holdings that had been consolidated, together with the names of those to which they were annexed, as well as with lists of labourers' cottages which are now uninhabited[1].

That either this process of consolidation must have been retarded, or that the increase in the number of "industrial small holdings" must have gone on apace, is shown by the fact that, already by 1905, there was an increase of over 360 in the total number of holdings under 50 acres. This process continued up to 1912, thus making an increase of 433 in the total number of small holdings during the 17 years after 1895. It is interesting to note that this period was, generally, one of comparative agricultural prosperity.

Since 1912 there has been a continuous annual decrease in the numbers of the 1 to 5 acre group. During the same period the respective fortunes of the two groups between 5 and 50 acres have been fairly similar. Taking first the 5 to 20 acre group, we find a continuous annual fall in the number of holdings down to the year 1917, after which there is an increase of 114 by 1921, when a definitely opposite movement seems to have set in again, resulting in a loss of 118 holdings in the next two years. Similarly, the number of holdings in the 20 to 50 acre group was increased by 157 between 1917 and 1921, while already by 1923 a fall of 53 holdings had been registered. This increase between 1917 and 1921, with the subsequent falling off that seems to have set in, may be taken

[1] C. 8221 (1896), *op. cit.* p. 355. Also, Minutes of Evidence: 38,499–38,505; 39,272; 39,458; 39,674; 40,270; 40,660; 42,058; 42,134; 42,686–42,705; 42,752–42,756.

as further evidence of the generally held opinion that the number of small holdings tends to increase during times of prosperity, and to decrease when conditions are less favourable.

From 1908 onwards the numbers of small holdings in the county have been somewhat affected as a result of legislative action by the County Council. Thus, up to the end of 1914, 47 small holdings were let, under the terms of the Small Holdings and Allotments Act of 1908[1]. Secondly, a colony of smallholders was created at Pembrey under the provisions of the Small Holdings Colonies Act of 1916[2]. Lastly, the Land Settlement (Facilities) Act of 1919 has resulted in the establishment of 77 ex-service men on small holdings in the county[3].

To sum up, it seems, from the official statistics, that there has not been a very pronounced change during the last 40 years in the total number of small holdings in the county. The percentage which holdings of 1 to 50 acres in extent have formed of the total number of holdings in the county at various periods is as follows:

1885	...	...	61·1 per cent.
1912	...	...	63·9 ,,
1923	...	...	63·6 ,,

These figures show that a large number of small peasant farms has been a constant feature of the agricultural economy of the county. A similar impression of constancy is obtained from a study of the total acreage which such

[1] *Annual Reports of Proceedings under the Small Holdings and Allotments Act*, 1908, part I, 1915 (Cd. 7851).

[2] *Report of Proceedings under the Small Holdings Colonies Acts* (1916 *and* 1918) *and the Sailors and Soldiers* (*Gift of Land Settlement*) *Act* 1916.

[3] *Report on Land Settlement in England and Wales*, 1919 *to* 1924, part 4, Table A.

small holdings have covered at different periods, the figures for which are as follows:

	Total acreage of 1 to 50 acre holdings	Do. as percentage of total acreage of holdings in the county
1885*	93,388	21·2
1912†	104,920	23·9
1919‡	105,744	24·8

* C. 4848. † Cd. 6597. ‡ Cmd. 680.

5. PRESENT DIVISION OF HOLDINGS

The present state of the division of agricultural holdings in the county is given in Table IV, which has been prepared to show the division into size groups according to the agricultural returns obtained on June 4th, 1923.

TABLE IV. Number and percentage distribution of agricultural holdings on June 4th, 1923[1]

Acres	No. of holdings	Percentage number
1–5	867	10·1
5–20	2369	27·7
20–50	2203	25·7
1–50	5439	63·5
50–100	1999	23·4
Over 100	1118	13·1
Total	8556	100·0

The table provides excellent evidence of the preponderance of the small farm in the economy of the county, 86·9 per cent. of all the holdings being under 100 acres in extent, and over 73 per cent. of these are small holdings in the more limited sense of the term. Both

[1] *Agricultural Statistics*, 1923, part I.

small allotment holdings and the larger farms are comparatively few in number. Thus, the 1 to 5 acre group contains only 10·1 per cent. of the total number of holdings, while only 13·1 per cent. are over 100 acres in extent.

As a preliminary to this survey an analysis was made of all the parish rate books in the county, in order to ascertain the numbers of small holdings on a parish basis. It is very interesting to compare the estimates thus obtained with the official estimates of the number of holdings in the county, and the two are given side by side in the following table:

Acres	Official estimates		Survey estimates *	
	Number	Percentage	Number	Percentage
1–20	3236	37·8	2284	32·1
20–50	2203	25·7	1803	25·3
50–100	1999	23·4	1629	22·9
Over 100	1118	13·1	1405	19·7
Total	8556	100·0	7121	100·0

* Holdings in the urban parishes of Ammanford and Llanelly and in the parish of Quarter Bach are not included.

While it is difficult to account satisfactorily for the very considerable difference between the two sets of figures, the following reasons have undoubtedly been partly responsible. In the first place, the numbers of smaller holdings given in the official statistics are liable to inflation by the practice of returning separately two or more holdings occupied by the same person, although, in actual practice, they are worked as a single undertaking[1]. In the survey statistics, error from this source is also possible, although precaution was taken to avoid multiplication of returns in the many cases where one agricultural unit is represented by more

[1] Vide *Agricultural Statistics*, 1922, part I, p. 12.

than one entry in the same rate book, or by entries in both rate books of adjoining parishes. A second reason may be found in the different methods of arriving at the size of holdings. In the one case, the simple entry of acreage in the parish rate books was used, while in the official statistics the area of rough grazings is eliminated from the size of the holding. Finally, the reliability of the acreages entered in the parish rate books is far from satisfactory, so that error from this source must be expected. These explanations agree somewhat with the fact that the greatest degree of discrepancy between the two estimates is in the number of small holdings given. Thus holdings between 1 and 50 acres are over 900 more according to the official statistics, while, on the other hand, holdings over 100 acres in extent are 287 more according to the survey estimates.

The exact position probably lies somewhere between these two sets of figures, and the examination would be useful were it only to show, once more, the need for a more careful and elaborate investigation into the statistics of the size of holdings in the country.

Unfortunately, official figures of the total acreage of holdings in each size group have not been given since 1919, when the position was as shown in the following table:

TABLE V. Acreage and percentage distribution of agricultural holdings in 1919[1]

Acres	Total acreage in group	Percentage of total acreage	Average size per holding
1–5	3,202	0·75	3·3
5–20	27,990	6·55	11·2
20–50	74,552	17·48	34·2
50–100	143,746	33·71	73·1
Over 100	176,894	41·51	148·6
Total	426,384	100·00	48·98

[1] Cmd. 680.

Nearly 60 per cent. of the total acreage accounted for is made up of holdings under 100 acres in extent, so that these groups are the most important, both as regards the number of holdings included, as well as the acreage covered. The average acreage per holding is also shown in the table, 48·98 acres being given as the average size of all holdings in the county.

6. TENURE OF SMALL HOLDINGS

The material obtained from the survey of the parish rate books can be used to illustrate the nature of the tenure of the small holdings in the county. The detailed analysis of this data, which is shown in Table VI, has

TABLE VI. Tenure of 4087 small holdings

| Acres | Total no. of holdings | No. owned or mainly owned | No. rented or mainly rented | | | | Percentage no. owned or mainly owned | Percentage no. rented or mainly rented |
| | | | No. owned by | | | Total | | |
			Private persons	County Council	Other public bodies			
1–10	1322	575	715	8	24	747	43·5	56·5
10–20	962	424	522	8	8	538	44·1	55·9
20–30	646	283	346	9	8	363	43·8	56·2
30–50	1157	535	581	33	8	622	46·2	53·8
1–50	4087	1817	2164	58	48	2270	44·4	55·6

been made possible through the co-operation of the Assistant Overseers of the various parishes, who were able to supplement the statistical evidence on tenure contained in the rate books by their intimate local knowledge.

It will be seen that, in each of the four size-groups, over 43 per cent. of the holdings are occupied by their owners[1]. The percentage of tenant occupiers is highest in the 1 to 10

[1] It is interesting to note that the proportion of owner occupiers in the sample of 262 small holdings taken in the survey tallies closely with the proportion given here. *Vide post*, p. 34.

acre group, but the difference from group to group is very slight. Only 2·6 per cent. of all the holdings are owned by public or corporate bodies; 58 of the 106 holdings so owned belong to the County Council, and the majority of the remaining 48 holdings are glebe property.

Here, again, it is necessary to draw attention to the very different picture which is presented by the official data on this question of tenure. The latest official statistics of the numbers of small holdings owned or mainly owned by their occupiers are those for 1922, when only 11·91 per cent. of all the holdings under 50 acres in extent were returned as occupied by their owners[1]. The agricultural statistics for 1923 show an increase of 40 per cent. in the number of such holdings for the whole of England and Wales, the figures for every county being larger than in 1922[2]. Unfortunately, the county figures are not given in the report, but, even assuming the increase to have been uniform for the whole country and for all groups, there would still be considerable discrepancy between the official estimates and the estimate given in Table VI. In the agricultural returns for 1924 particular attention is drawn to the difficulty of obtaining accurate information on this subject of ownership[3], and, from what is said

[1] *Agricultural Statistics*, 1922, part I, Table VIII.
[2] *Agricultural Statistics*, 1923, part I.
[3] *Agricultural Statistics*, 1924, part I, p. 13: "A very large proportion of the 1924 returns were compared with those for the same holdings in 1923. Although there is no obvious reason why this question on the schedule should not be correctly answered, the examination showed a number of cases where the statements made by the same person in respect of the same holding were such as to give rise to doubt as to their accuracy, while in about one-third the question was unanswered...on the whole it was obvious that a considerable margin of error existed, and it is possible that the number of holdings owned or partly owned is larger than is shown in the Table... the fact whether an occupier does or does not own the whole or part of his holding, though it may be known locally by report, is a matter which must depend on the voluntary statement of the occupier."

there, it does seem that, here at least, the survey estimates approximate more nearly to the actual state of affairs.

What is quite certain is that during the last few years there has been a marked increase in the percentage of occupying owners for all groups throughout the country. But, before the full significance of the position can be appreciated, much more information must be forthcoming as to the true financial status of these new owners. Here the official statistics are silent, since, not only is there no information as to the degree of mortgage obtaining on the farms of the country, but no register is kept of the changes that occur in the ownership of these farms. There can be no doubt, therefore, that some simple system of land registration—either the registration of deeds as practised in most European countries, or registration of title as practised in the British Dominions—would be to the public interest[1].

7. GEOGRAPHICAL DISTRIBUTION OF SMALL HOLDINGS

The estimates obtained from the parish rate books can be further utilised to show the geographical distribution of the holdings in the county. For this purpose the 85 parishes in the county have been divided between the seven Poor Law Unions, and Table VII gives the number of holdings per size-group, together with their percentage distribution for each of these seven divisions.

The most striking feature of the table is the marked similarity which is shown to exist in the distribution of holdings for the various districts. Small farms under 100 acres in extent form nearly 80 per cent. of the holdings in six of the divisions. The highest percentage of such

[1] *Agricultural Tribunal of Investigation*, Cmd. 2145 (1924), Final Report, pp. 38–40.

TABLE VII. Geographical distribution of holdings
compiled in unions

Union	1–10 acres	10–20 acres	20–30 acres	30–50 acres	50–100 acres	over 100 acres	Total
Carmarthen	410 *18·2%*	299 *13·2%*	211 *9·3%*	385 *17·0%*	536 *23·7%*	424 *18·7%*	2265 *100·0%*
Llandeilo	197 *16·6%*	196 *16·4%*	140 *11·7%*	203 *17·0%*	280 *23·5%*	177 *14·8%*	1193 *100·0%*
Llanelly	159 *21·7%*	107 *14·6%*	68 *9·3%*	143 *19·5%*	177 *24·1%*	79 *10·8%*	733 *100·0%*
Llandovery	143 *12·4%*	102 *8·9%*	73 *6·3%*	187 *16·2%*	284 *24·7%*	363 *31·5%*	1152 *100·0%*
Lampeter	188 *25·1%*	115 *15·3%*	47 *6·3%*	106 *14·1%*	154 *20·5%*	140 *18·7%*	750 *100·0%*
N. C. Emlyn	136 *29·6%*	66 *14·4%*	44 *9·6%*	49 *10·7%*	88 *19·1%*	76 *16·6%*	459 *100·0%*
Narberth	89 *15·6%*	77 *13·5%*	63 *11·1%*	84 *14·8%*	110 *19·3%*	146 *25·7%*	569 *100·0%*
County Totals	1322 *18·6%*	962 *13·5%*	646 *9·1%*	1157 *16·2%*	1629 *22·9%*	1405 *19·7%*	7121 *100·0%*

farms obtains for the Llanelly division, which has all its
parishes situated in the industrial area. Similarly, four of
the parishes in the Llandeilo area, which comes next, are
also mainly industrial. At the other extreme is the
Llandovery Union, which has more than 31 per cent. of
its holdings over 100 acres in extent. This area corresponds
with the more mountainous north-west portion of the
county, where the number of extensive sheep walks is responsible for the relatively higher percentage of large farms.

　　It is interesting to note the marked similarity in the
movements in the number of small holdings from group
to group, both in the county as a whole, and in each of
the seven divisions. Thus, there is a fall in the number

of holdings from the first group to the second, and a further fall to the third group, after which there is an increase in the 30 to 50 acre group, followed by a further increase in the 50 to 100 acre group. This movement is significant, inasmuch as the comparative unpopularity, in point of numbers, of the intermediate groups may reflect the existence of an uneconomic holding, which, on the one hand, is too cumbersome as an allotment, and, on the other, is too meagre for the full-time employment and sustenance of its occupier. More light will be thrown on this problem of the auxiliary small holding by the following analysis of the employment of the occupiers of small holdings in the county.

8. EMPLOYMENT CENSUS OF THE OCCUPIERS OF SMALL HOLDINGS

All serious discussions of the small holdings problem have recognised the necessity for distinguishing between holding which give full-time employment to their occupiers, and holdings which are only used as adjuncts to other businesses. The problem of the first type of holding is the real small holdings problem, while the other is, really, the problem of the allotment, and the allotment holding. In spite of this important difference, however, there is practically no available statistical information as to what number, or what proportion, of the smaller holdings are occupied by people who follow other occupations, to whom farming is only of secondary importance. For England and Wales there are no official statistics whatever on this subject, while the few personal enquiries that have been made have been very restricted in their scope[1].

[1] See, for example, Ashby, *op. cit.* p. 126; J. Pryse-Howell, *An Economic Survey of a Rural Parish* (Oxford University Press), appendix 2.

Some foreign countries, on the other hand, consider information on this point to be of sufficient importance for inclusion in their periodic agricultural statistics[1].

Inasmuch as information of this nature forms a necessary introduction to the present investigation, an attempt was made to ascertain the nature of the employment of the occupiers of the 4087 small holdings registered in the parish rate books. The details in every case were obtained by personal enquiry, and, here again, the ready co-operation of the Assistant Overseers was invaluable. An analysis of the results thus obtained is set out in detail in the following table:

TABLE VIII. Employment of 4087 smallholders

Acres	No. of holdings	No. with farming as only employment				No. with additional employment	Percentage no. with farming as only employment	Percentage no. with additional employment
		Retired persons or pensioners	Women	Others	Total			
1–10	1322	132	257	59	448	874	33·9	66·1
10–20	962	93	164	157	414	548	43·0	57·0
20–30	646	23	77	275	375	271	58·0	42·0
30–50	1157	0	114	831	945	212	81·7	18·3
1–50	4087	248	612	1322	2182	1905	54·1	45·9

The percentage of occupiers with no other employment than farming is seen to increase from group to group—from 33·9 per cent. in the 1 to 10 acre group to 81·7 per cent. in the 30 to 50 acre group. However, the number of *bona fide* smallholders (i.e. those entirely occupied on their holdings, and deriving full sustenance therefrom) must be regarded as restricted to the column headed

[1] *Vide post*, Appendix C, footnote 1, p. 106.

"Others" in the table. Only 4·5 per cent. of the holdings in the 1 to 10 acre group are occupied by such people, and most of these are market gardeners or poultry farmers; the 10 to 20 acre group contains 11·9 per cent., and the 20 to 30 acre group 20·8 per cent. A considerable number of retired farmers are found as occupiers of the smaller holdings, which shows that this unit has its place at the top, as well as at the foot, of the so-called "agricultural ladder." The high number of women occupiers, particularly on the larger holdings, illustrates the general case in Wales of the comparatively higher proportion of women in occupation of farms. This is "more than a slight indication that the continuance of farms on the death of the occupier as family holdings was more general in Wales than in other parts of the Kingdom."[1]

A movement converse to the above with increase in the size of holdings is manifested in the percentage of occupiers having some employment in addition to agriculture. Thus, while 66·1 per cent. of the occupiers of holdings from 1 to 10 acres in extent have some other business, the corresponding figure for the occupiers of the 30 to 50 acre group is only 18·3 per cent. Nearly 50 per cent. of all holdings under 50 acres in extent are occupied by persons with non-agricultural employments, and in Table IX a detailed analysis of these employments is given. The greater portion of those shown as "general labourers" in the table are farm employees. Strictly speaking, therefore, they should not be included with those described as being engaged in "non-agricultural" trades. This has been done, however, since they also are not entirely dependent on their holdings for their subsistence.

[1] C. 8221 (1896), *op. cit.* p. 149

TABLE IX. Employment of 1905 smallholders engaged in non-agricultural occupations

	1–10 (acres)	10–20 (acres)	20–30 (acres)	30–50 (acres)	1–50 (acres)
General labourers	159	122	58	21	360
Road labourers	54	31	16	9	110
Hauliers	13	21	20	24	78
Woodmen	9	7	2	1	19
Gardeners	3	4	1	0	8
Blacksmiths	29	19	7	3	58
Carpenters, wheelwrights, etc.	59	33	18	14	124
Masons	24	19	8	4	55
Shoemakers and cobblers ...	6	6	2	1	15
Clogmakers ...	1	4	0	2	7
Coopers and hoopers ...	3	0	0	0	3
Tailors	10	2	1	2	15
Weavers	22	4	3	0	29
Dyers	1	0	0	0	1
Rabbit catchers	7	4	1	0	12
Gamekeepers	1	0	1	0	2
Jockeys and horse trainers	3	2	0	0	5
Coachmen and chauffeurs ...	5	0	1	0	6
Butchers	29	20	12	11	72
Bakers	1	0	1	0	2
Millers	23	13	7	8	51
Publicans	48	19	13	12	92
Grocers and provision dealers	48	17	6	6	77
Cattle dealers and hucksters	24	16	9	18	67
Milk vendors	6	7	3	7	23
Woollen manufacturers ...	26	5	1	1	33
Tanyard proprietors ...	1	1	0	2	4
Coal merchants ...	6	0	0	0	6
Timber merchants ...	2	11	3	8	24
Ministers of religion ...	28	7	6	5	46
Medical practitioners ...	2	0	0	0	2
Schoolmasters	2	2	1	0	5
Veterinary surgeons ...	0	0	2	1	3
Auctioneers, surveyors, etc.	7	7	5	2	21
Postal employees	8	7	2	1	18
Parochial officers	8	2	0	2	12
Clerks	8	3	2	0	13
Clockmakers	1	0	0	0	1
Piano tuners	1	0	0	0	1
Hairdressers	1	0	0	0	1
Cockledealers and fishermen	2	2	0	0	4
Coal miners	150	117	53	43	363
Tinplate workers ...	6	1	1	0	8
Lime workers	1	0	1	0	2
Railwaymen	16	10	3	4	33
Quarrymen	10	3	1	0	14
Totals	874	548	271	212	1905

In order to complete this analysis, the 1905 holdings, whose occupiers follow non-agricultural pursuits, should have been divided into two groups according as to whether they supplement their occupiers' other employments, or whether those employments supplement the tenure of the holdings. Unfortunately the information is not sufficiently complete to enable this to be done. Nevertheless, Table IX illustrates the present importance of the small holding to the country labourer, the village artisan and the village tradesman, while it is patronised also by the village divine[1]. It is interesting to suggest, here, some connection between certain occupations and their need for land. For example, the hauliers, the shopkeepers, the hucksters, and the carriers often need the land to graze the horses which they employ in their various occupations. In the case of the labourers and the artisans, the lure of keeping one or two cows is probably a greater factor. The butchers and the cattle dealers need accommodation land, while the village publican often depends as much on his holding as on the proceeds of his licensed trade. The use of the small

[1] It is instructive to compare Table IX with the following analysis of the occupations of the 386 applicants for County Council small holdings in the county from 1908 to 1914:

No.	Occupation	No.	Occupation	No.	Occupation
140	Farmers	6	Millers	3	Veterinary surgeons
45	Colliers	6	Butchers	2	Postmen
27	Farm labourers	6	Women	2	Tailors
20	Shopkeepers, etc.	5	Milk vendors	2	Fishermen [turers
15	General labourers	5	Gardeners	2	Woollen manufac-
14	Carpenters	5	Woodmen	2	Colliery managers
11	Hauliers	5	Blacksmiths	1	Poultry farmer
8	Railwaymen	5	Bootmakers	1	Horse trainer
8	Weavers	5	Jobbers	1	Piano tuner
7	Road labourers	3	Quarrymen	1	Relieving officer
7	Publicans	3	Coal merchants	1	Garage proprietor
7	Masons				

holding by the industrial worker has already been noted; it is well illustrated in the table by the large number of holdings, in each of the four groups, which are occupied by miners from the extensive coal area located within the county.

The economics of these adjunctive holdings forms a study in itself. Together with specialised holdings they are, therefore, excluded from the present work, which limits itself to an examination of the economic position of the small "family farm" holding on which the occupier is fully employed, and from which he expects to derive his whole livelihood. This small, economic, farm holding—which, it is believed, is the main small holding problem—has been shown to be the prevalent type in the past, as well as in the present agricultural economy of the county.

SECTION III

ECONOMIC CONDITIONS OF CARMARTHEN-SHIRE SMALLHOLDERS

A. METHOD OF INVESTIGATION

The two chief methods that have been used in the study of farm economics are the "accountancy method" and the "survey method." The accountancy method involves an exact study of economic phenomena based on careful and elaborate records of the organisation and business transactions of certain selected farms. Although the primary purpose of this method is to give the farmer himself information as to what to produce, and how to produce it in order to secure the maximum advantage from the undertaking, it can also have general value, e.g. in discovering the range of costs of producing each of the various farm products, and in discovering the distribution of the agricultural income within the industry. In this country, on the other hand, the survey method is used when less accurate information is required, and it aims at covering much larger areas and longer periods of time than can be conveniently covered by the keeping of accounts. Thus, it yields useful information on such problems as systems of farming, distribution of holdings, labour organisation, efficiency of farm equipment, and general housing conditions; it is also well adapted for the study of the interrelation of physical or social conditions and farming practices. In short, the survey method gives "breadth of view and a basis for sound judgment as to the trend of affairs. The accountancy method gives depth of insight and the basis of keen analysis."[1]

Both these methods have been used to a certain extent in the present investigation. The analysis divides itself accordingly into two sections—the one based on an extensive survey of 262 small holdings in the county, the other on a more intensive study based on financial accounts kept by a sample of 93 of these smallholders.

The technique of the investigation was briefly as follows. A number of representative smallholders was selected in every parish, to whom a preliminary schedule of questions was forwarded. The schedule, which indicated the general nature of the information required, was collected during a personal visit which followed within a few days after its dispatch. The intrinsic value of the schedule itself was subsidiary to its importance as a valuable preparation for the subsequent personal visit, when further information was solicited on all possible details of the economy of the holdings. With very few exceptions this information was given to the utmost ability of the occupiers, and everywhere the inquirer was received with intelligent kindness and given every assistance. The data collected in this manner are the raw material on which the results described in the second part of this section are based.

A certain number of the more responsive of these smallholders was also persuaded to keep simple financial records of their holdings for the period of one year, and for this purpose they were supplied with ordinary account books in which they were instructed to enter details of all their purchases and sales. The contents of these simple financial accounts are analysed in detail in the last part of this section.

[1] *The Place of Economics in Agricultural Education and Research*, by H. C. Taylor (The University of Wisconsin Agricultural Experiment Station, Research Bulletin No. 16, 1911), p. 107.

B. ANALYSIS OF A SURVEY OF 262 SMALL HOLDINGS

1. CLASSIFICATION OF HOLDINGS

Although the main object of this survey was to obtain a general impression of the small holdings in the county, it was felt that the information collected, if properly classified, could also be used for studying more general economic problems. But this question of suitable classification of holdings is difficult, on account of the many possible methods which suggest themselves, such as altitude, size, rent, ownership, etc.—and each of these possesses its peculiar advantages for the exploration of the various problems which might be pursued. But considerations of space and labour make impossible the use of all these; accordingly, for this study, a classification based solely on altitude and acreage has been employed. Such a classification is at once simple and capable of bringing out fairly clearly the main reliefs of the survey. The division on an acreage basis lends itself admirably to a discussion of the correlation between the size of the holding and its economic characteristics. Acreage alone, however, can only be a satisfactory basis for classification when the geographical features of the area surveyed are fairly uniform. In the present study, therefore, the introduction of altitude gives due weight to an important distinction which necessarily exists between highland and lowland farms whether they be large or small. Five hundred feet above sea level has been adopted as the dividing line between these two types of highland and lowland holdings. Such a classification based on acreage and altitude is shown in Table X, where the 262 small holdings of the survey are divided accordingly into six groups.

TABLE X. Classification of 262 small holdings

Class		No. of holdings	Total acreage	Average size per holding (acres)	Average rental per acre
					£ *s.* *d.*
A. *Highland holdings:*					
(1) Under 30 acres	...	19	441	23·2	1 2 1
(2) 30 to 60 acres	...	64	2664	41·6	17 0
(3) Over 60 acres	...	17	1549	91·0	9 9
All highland holdings	...	100	4654	46·5	14 9
B. *Lowland holdings:*					
(1) Under 25 acres	...	27	539	19·9	1 17 3
(2) 25 to 50 acres	...	105	3958	37·6	1 11 0
(3) Over 50 acres	...	30	1799	59·6	1 9 2
All lowland holdings	...	162	6296	38·9	1 10 5

It will be noticed that the two main acreage divisions are slightly different, the average holding being smaller for the various groups in the lowlands than it is for the corresponding highland groups. This is the result of an attempt to take into consideration the quality as well as the quantity of the land. And, in order to show this more clearly, the average rentals per acre for the various groups are also given in the table. These figures of rent are largely estimates, since, in the case of occupying owners, the rent is necessarily an arbitrary figure based, either, on the previous rental of the holding, or, on the assessment made by the occupier himself[1]. Nevertheless, the figures illustrate

[1] The percentage of occupying owners was as follows for the various groups:

Group A 1 ...   42 %   Group B 1 ...   52 %
„   A 2 ...   48 %   „   B 2 ...   45 %
„   A 3 ...   47 %   „   B 3 ...   40 %

These figures should be compared with those quoted in the discussion on tenure on pp. 21–23.

a tendency that has been corroborated by every study of the influence of the size of holding, viz. a fall in rental per acre as the size of the holding rises, which is shown to be common to both highland and lowland groups.

2. CROPS

In the Introduction to this study Carmarthenshire farming was described as being predominantly pastoral. It will be seen, therefore, from the next table that the small holdings included in this survey are, in this respect at least, typical of the county as a whole. The table gives a detailed analysis of the total area surveyed, and shows the actual area as well as the percentage of permanent pasture, arable land, and rough grazings.

TABLE XI. Distribution of area

	Total acreage	Acreage rough pasture	Percentage rough pasture	Acreage permanent grazing	Percentage permanent grazing	Acreage kept for hay	Percentage kept for hay	Acreage arable land	Percentage arable land
Group A 1	441	4	1·0	282	64·0	105	23·7	50	11·3
„ A 2	2664	254	9·5	1389	52·1	621	23·4	400	15·0
„ A 3	1549	510	32·9	628	40·6	211	13·6	200	12·9
Groups A 1–A 3	4654	768	16·5	2299	49·6	937	20·1	650	13·8
Group B 1	539	—	—	339	63·0	188	34·8	12	2·2
„ B 2	3958	112	2·8	2317	58·6	1264	31·9	265	6·7
„ B 3	1799	44	2·4	1022	56·8	588	32·7	145	8·1
Groups B 1–B 3	6296	156	2·5	3678	58·5	2040	32·3	422	6·7

The table shows that over 80 per cent. of the land in all the groups is under grass, and, with the exception of the third highland group, very little of this is under rough grazing. The pasture land varies considerably in quality, and although many good pastures are found, there are large areas which are capable of considerable improvement. Unfortunately very little is done towards improving the poorer fields, and where artificial manures are used they are applied to the better pasture land. On these basic slag is freely used and they are chain harrowed and rolled in the spring.

As hay forms the mainstay of the winter feed, the hay fields are very important on all the holdings. The bulk of the farmyard manure produced is applied to them, and thus a dressing per acre of from 12 to 15 loads of dung is given every three or four years, while sometimes in the intermediate years from 5 to 6 cwt. of basic slag is also applied. Generally the same fields are kept for hay year after year, and it would probably improve the quality of the herbage if they were grazed and mowed alternately. Over 20 per cent. of the total area of the highland holdings and over 32 per cent. of the lowland holdings are under hay, and the yield varies from 15 to 20 cwt. per acre.

Both the hay fields and the pasture land would benefit by a more general application of lime. Very little liming is done at present, and recent soil analyses made in the county reveal a general deficiency in lime.

The small area of arable land, which is generally confined to a few convenient fields near the homestead, accounts for less than 10 per cent. of the total area of all the holdings, while many holdings, particularly in the lowlands, have no arable land at all[1]. The higher percentage of arable shown to obtain for the highlands is due probably

---

[1] The percentage number of holdings with no arable land is as follows for the various groups:

Group A 1 ...	31·6 %	Group B 1 ...	74·0 %
„ A 2 ...	6·3 %	„ B 2 ...	44·8 %
„ A 3 ...	0·0 %	„ B 3 ...	13·3 %

to the poorer quality of the soil, making it necessary to grow crops for the sustenance of live stock, while ploughing and re-sowing also is needed often for the maintenance of a good turf.

The systems of cropping are very indefinite, and many modifications of the four course rotation are practised, of which the following is the most general—oats or wheat, oats, roots, and seeds. The acreage of the various crops grown per 100 acres arable land is given in the following table:

TABLE XII. Acreage of crops grown per 100 acres arable land

	Wheat	Oats	Barley	Dredge corn	Total cereals	Potatoes	Turnips	Swedes	Mangolds	Cabbage plants	Total potatoes, green crops, etc.
Group A 1	0	52	22	15	89	7	0·7	2·0	1·0	0·3	11
„ A 2	6	47	12	20	85	8	0·5	3·5	2·5	0·5	15
„ A 3	6	58	8	14	86	7	1·0	3·5	2·5	0·0	14
Groups A 1–A 3	4	52	14	17	87	7	0·7	3·0	2·0	0·3	13
Group B 1	0	42	0	9	51	19	0	6	10	14	49
„ B 2	4	46	11	13	74	12	5	4	4	1	26
„ B 3	6	42	10	20	78	9	4	5	3	1	22
Groups B 1–B 3	3	43	7	14	67	14	3	5	6	5	33

Oats is by far the most important cereal crop, barley and dredge corn, a mixture of barley and oats, coming next, while hardly any wheat is grown. The potato crop is important since it forms such a large portion of the diet of the family, and potatoes are also fed extensively to the pigs. The entire root crop is seen to be insignificant, swedes and mangolds being mostly grown. There is practically no bare fallow.

It is perfectly clear, therefore, that arable cultivation is of secondary importance in the economy of the small holdings investigated. Moreover, practically the whole of the produce of the small arable area obtaining is consumed on the holdings themselves.

3. LIVE STOCK

The live stock economy, on the other hand, covers practically the whole of the activities of the smallholders. Consequently the greater part of the data collected during the survey is concerned with the live stock equipment of the holdings. The figures in the tables which follow have been obtained by weighting the numbers of the maximum stock by the period of time such stock are actually on the holding. An example will make the method clear—a herd of milch cows is returned as 10, since this number is on the holding throughout the year; on the other hand, if 6 of the calves are sold at 2 months old, they are returned as being equivalent to 1 calf on the holding throughout the year. In this way it is believed that a better indication is obtained of the real "stock carrying capacity" of the holdings than would be the case if the numbers of the stock at its maximum strength had been taken[1].

(a) *Cattle.* Inasmuch as the raising of store cattle and the production of dairy produce are the chief pursuits, most of the herds kept are of the dual purpose type. The great majority of them are non-pedigree Shorthorns, a few Welsh Black Cattle are found in the south of the county on the Pembrokeshire border, while on four of the holdings in the Llandovery district Herefords were kept. Unfortunately many of the herds, particularly in the highlands,

[1] For further use of this method see "An Economic Survey of a Farming District in the Thames Valley," by J. Pryse-Howell (unpublished).

are of a very inferior type. However, through the facilities offered by the Live Stock Scheme of the Ministry of Agriculture and Fisheries, good work is being done in the county towards improving the quality of the live stock. The smallholder, by being assisted to keep only the most economic type of animal, stands to gain most from the scheme, since where the scale of the undertaking is small the efficiency of each item of production becomes proportionately more important.

The detail of the head of cattle per 100 acres is as follows:

TABLE XIII. Head of cattle per 100 acres

	Cows	Bulls	Two year old cattle	Yearlings	Calves	Total
Group A 1	18·6	0·0	5·2	5·2	9·1	38·1
„ A 2	13·1	0·5	3·7	6·3	9·2	32·8
„ A 3	6·8	0·4	2·8	5·4	5·4	20·8
Groups A 1–A 3	11·7	0·4	3·5	5·5	7·9	29·0
Group B 1	26·7	0·3	5·6	7·2	7·4	47·2
„ B 2	21·8	1·5	5·5	10·0	10·1	48·9
„ B 3	20·2	1·4	4·0	6·6	8·9	41·1
Groups B 1–B 3	21·8	1·4	5·1	8·2	9·5	46·0

The table shows a general tendency for the head of cattle per 100 acres to decrease with the size of the holding as well as with the altitude. This tendency is perfectly regular for the mature stock, but in the case of yearlings and calves there is an increase from the first to the second group in both highland and lowland holdings, and this is due to the very limited stock rearing practised on the smaller farms. The figures are necessary reflections of the various systems of management, the chief modifications being due to the relative importance of dairying and stock raising. In order to illustrate this further, Table XIV has been prepared to show the relative importance of the three dairy products in the economy of the holdings.

TABLE XIV. Percentage of holdings selling milk and butter, and making cheese

	Percentage holdings selling milk	Percentage holdings selling butter	Percentage holdings making cheese
Group A 1	0	100	58
„ A 2	0	100	56
„ A 3	0	100	71
Group B 1	22	82	33
„ B 2	30	75	41
„ B 3	53	50	33

The making of butter for sale, which is first in importance, was practised on all the highland holdings, as well as on 71 per cent. of the lowland holdings. The selling of whole milk is necessarily restricted to those districts which are best served by transport facilities. These coincide for the greater part with the valleys, so that this practice is limited entirely to the lowland holdings. Most of the holdings selling milk retain sufficient for the consumption by the family of milk and butter. Only 6 holdings were found where the entire milk supply was sold and the butter for the household bought in. The production of cheese has dwindled considerably during the last two decades, a tendency that has synchronised with the advent of the centrifugal separator. Nevertheless, the table shows that there is still considerable production of cheese for home consumption, a practice which obtained on 62 per cent. of the highland, and on 38 per cent. of the lowland holdings. On 11 holdings only was cheese made for sale.

Next in importance to dairying comes the rearing of store cattle, which was practised to some extent on most of the holdings. Most of the calves are reared and sold as stores at ages varying from eighteen months to two years, one or two in-calf heifers being retained for replenishing the milch herd when necessary. In the case of the milk-selling holdings, however, most of the calves are sold when a few days old; one or two heifer calves are kept and reared for the herd, but quite often all the calves are sold, the herd being replenished entirely by buying in-calf heifers or cows. Generally there is very little fattening done, but if circumstances are favourable the small farmer will fatten an occasional barren cow or perhaps a promising young bullock.

The number of cattle sold per 100 acres was as follows:

TABLE XV. Number of cattle sold per 100 acres

	Cows	Two-year old cattle and yearlings	Calves	Total
Group A 1 ...	5·2	5·0	8·6	18·8
„ A 2 ...	3·7	5·4	4·2	13·3
„ A 3 ...	2·8	2·6	2·1	7·5
Group B 1 ...	8·2	1·9	19·3	29·4
„ B 2 ...	5·9	5·0	11·1	22·0
„ B 3 ...	4·7	4·9	12·6	22·2

Unfortunately it is not possible to give separately the numbers of store cattle and of fat stock sold. However, so far as sales can be taken as an indication of production, the table shows an inverse ratio between the production and the size of the holding for both highland and lowland groups. It also shows the superior gross production per acre on the lowland holdings.

(b) *Horses*. The problem of horse labour is one of the most serious which the smallholder has to face. In the first place, the capital invested in horses (like the capital invested in machinery) may be idle for considerable periods. Secondly, a horse on the small holding can always be regarded as supplanting a potential cow—a far more profitable unit of production. Two methods, both of which are practised, whereby the smallholder can partly meet this difficulty are—either, by undertaking outside work such as haulage, or, by co-operation with his neighbours in the use of horse labour during certain busy seasons.

The horses usually kept on these holdings are the vanner and the collier type. The latter is from 14 to 15 hands high, with a good strong body and bone; it is well adapted for the work of the highland small holding, while there is always a market for it since it is also very suitable for work in the coal mines. On the lowland holdings a higher percentage of lighter horses such as cobs and ponies are kept, and these are suited for work in the lighter vehicles such as traps and milk floats which are more extensively used here. The next table gives the number of horses per 100 acres; it also gives the percentage of one-horse holdings, as well as the percentage of holdings on which brood mares are kept.

The figures in Table XVI must be read with some care, since, at the time of the survey, the horse management of many of the holdings was disorganised. This was the result of the slump in the horse trade then obtaining, in consequence of which many smallholders with colts and yearlings for sale had postponed selling in the hope of a better market coming. Nevertheless, the table helps to illustrate certain features of the horse economy of the small holdings. In the first place it shows that the highest number of horses per 100 acres is kept on the intermediate groups in both highlands and lowlands. The more favourable position in this respect on the smaller holdings is due to the fact that on most of these only one horse is kept, while on about 15 per cent. of the holdings in the first group in both highlands and lowlands there were no horses at all. Horsebreeding is not important in the county, and

TABLE XVI. Number of horses per 100 acres

	Draught horses	Two-year old horses	Yearlings	Foals	Total no. of horses	Percentage of one-horse holdings	Percentage holdings with brood mares
Group A 1	3·8	0·0	0·0	1·1	4·9	84	26
„ A 2	4·4	0·1	0·2	1·5	6·2	20	65
„ A 3	2·7	0·0	0·6	0·7	4·0	0	64
Groups A 1–A 3	3·8	0·0	0·3	1·2	5·3	32	58
Group B 1	5·0	0·0	0·0	1·7	6·7	88	33
„ B 2	4·3	0·2	1·3	1·5	7·3	15	55
„ B 3	3·9	0·4	1·3	1·3	6·9	0	80
Groups B 1–B 3	4·1	0·3	1·2	1·4	7·0	35	51

it is not suited to the economy of the smaller size of holding. Still, many of the smallholders keep a brood mare, and this helps them to a certain extent to meet the high cost of horse labour when the market is in a fairly prosperous state. The table shows that brood mares were kept on about 50 per cent. of the holdings visited, the percentage increasing rapidly with the increase in the size of the holding.

(c) *Sheep.* The two most common conditions for successful sheep farming—a large flock and a large run—make it unsuitable for the small holding. Nevertheless, the next table shows that the sheep is by no means absent from the holdings visited.

TABLE XVII. Number of sheep per 100 acres

	Breeding ewes	Rams	Yearlings	Lambs	Total	°/₀ holdings keeping sheep
Group A 1	13·6	0·7	2·7	10·9	27·9	37
„ A 2	18·8	1·0	6·4	15·0	41·2	55
„ A 3	42·9	1·2	10·6	27·2	81·9	94
Groups A 1–A 3	26·3	1·1	7·5	18·7	53·6	57
Group B 1	0·0	0·0	0·0	0·0	0·0	0
„ B 2	7·5	0·5	2·2	7·3	17·5	31
„ B 3	10·0	0·6	3·0	10·6	24·2	63
Groups B 1–B 3	7·5	0·5	2·3	7·6	17·9	29

The table gives the numbers of sheep kept per 100 acres, it also gives the percentage number of holdings in each group on which sheep are found. It will be seen that more sheep are kept on the larger than on the smaller holdings, and in the highlands than in the lowlands.

Most of the sheep are cross-bred. In the highlands the Welsh Mountain breed makes up the majority of the sheep population, while the Suffolk, Ryeland, and Kerry Hill type are more evident in the lowlands.

The usual system of sheep management on the lowland holdings is to keep a small flock of about a dozen breeding ewes. Lambing commences as early as January, lasting till the end of May. Most of the lambs are fattened on grass and sold usually from May to August, but some are kept as late as October. They are usually sold at live weights ranging from 80 to 100 pounds. On some of the holdings the ewes are bought in autumn, and sold with their lambs in spring; while the opposite system of buying the ewes early in spring and selling them and their lambs in autumn also obtains. Many smallholders, who do not keep a breeding flock, will buy in an occasional lot of lambs for fattening when the pasture is available.

On the highland holdings, however, far larger flocks are kept. There the lambing season is considerably later, and does not start until the end of March. The lambs are also sold off much later, often as late as the end of November, or they may be kept over the winter to be sold as yearlings in the following spring. In the vicinity of the Black Mountains an interesting custom of management prevails. Many of the smallholders share with the larger farmers extensive rights to common pasture on the mountains. This, combined with the "tacking system," enables large flocks of sheep to be kept which are hardly ever on the cultivated land. A typical example included in the survey will illustrate the custom. A flock of 65 breeding ewes was kept on a holding of 48 acres, carrying with it right of pasture to the Black Mountains. The ewes belong to the hardy breed of Welsh Mountain Sheep and lamb singly, roaming on the mountains with their lambs in summer. In autumn about two-thirds of the lambs and the oldest ewes are sold. The others are sent for the winter to Cardiganshire, where they are kept by the small farmers, who receive a fee of 10*s*. to 12*s*. per head of sheep wintered. This is the system of "tacking," and the period of the "tack" is usually from October to April.

On both highland and lowland holdings folding of sheep on arable land is very rare, the flocks being kept almost entirely on grass land, and very little cake or meal feeding is done.

(d) *Pigs*. Unlike sheep, the pig is generally considered

to be particularly adapted to the small holding. Pigs were found on every holding visited, and this is to say that every smallholder has his baconer for the household. Often, if the size of his family demands it, he will keep more than one pig for home consumption; this was actually the case on 52 of the holdings visited, where two pigs weighing from 13 to 20 score were slaughtered for the house. This "baconer for the house" will be a very important factor later on in estimating the standard of living of the smallholder.

The great majority of pigs are cross-bred. Black-coloured pigs are in disrepute in the county, and the more common crosses have been obtained by using the Large Whites, Middle Whites and Gloucester Spots. The native Welsh Pig is also used and the recent formation of the "Welsh Pig Society" may have important results in the county. The average number of pigs per 100 acres on the holdings throughout the year was as follows:

TABLE XVIII. Number of pigs per 100 acres

	Breeding sows	Pigs reared	Pigs bought	Total
Group A 1	3·4	11·1	4·6	19·1
,, A 2	1·8	7·6	2·4	11·8
,, A 3	1·1	4·1	0·8	6·0
Groups A 1–A 3	1·7	6·7	2·1	10·5
Group B 1	2·6	11·5	6·5	20·6
,, B 2	2·4	12·1	5·2	19·7
,, B 3	1·7	6·0	1·9	9·6
Groups B 1–B 3	2·2	10·3	4·4	16·9

This table illustrates the inverse ratio of the head of pigs per 100 acres and the size of the holding. It also shows that breeding sows are comparatively more numerous in the highlands, while in the lowlands more pigs are bought in. This is probably to be explained by the greater proximity to markets which the lowland farmer enjoys. Where breeding sows are kept, the progeny are sold either as weaners or as porkers, depending on the relative advantages of the market for these. On the other hand, where breeding sows are not kept, several lots of weaners may be bought annually to be sold later on as porkers and occasionally as baconers. According to the data, breeding sows were kept on 13 of the holdings, while the custom of buying in and feeding was practised on 80 other holdings. Only 30 holdings were found from which no pigs were sold. The next table gives the number of pigs sold per 100 acres.

TABLE XIX. Number of pigs sold per 100 acres

	Pigs reared			Pigs bought		Total
	Weaners	Porkers	Baconers	Porkers	Baconers	
Group A 1	22·2	6·3	0	9·3	1·1	38·9
,, A 2	30·7	4·2	0	4·7	0·9	40·5
,, A 3	16·3	2·1	0	0·0	0·6	19·0
Group B 1	69·4	4·1	0	14·8	0·9	89·2
,, B 2	35·8	5·8	0	14·0	0·3	55·9
,, B 3	25·8	2·6	2	3·6	1·0	35·0

This table agrees with what has been said above, and shows that a comparatively greater number of the pigs sold from the lowlands have not been bred on the holdings. It also shows that, for all groups, the sale of weaners and porkers is far more important than the sale of baconers.

(e) *Poultry*. Poultry are also generally admitted to be particularly adapted to the small farm, but, unfortunately, poultry are often treated by the smallholders themselves as of secondary importance in the undertaking. The proof of this is that far too many of the birds kept are of the "barn door" type, while other prevalent drawbacks are, the absence of scientific feeding, and the absence of adequately equipped poultry houses. Nevertheless, better conditions prevail on many holdings in both highlands and lowlands, where endeavours are made to improve the quality of the stock, the method of feeding, and the housing conditions. Progress in all these respects is undoubtedly accelerated by the educational work in the county, and by the activities of the twelve Egg and Chick Distributing Stations established under the Ministry of Agriculture's Scheme. The production of eggs for sale is the predominant object for which poultry are kept, the production of table poultry being practised on only a few holdings.

The details of the number of poultry kept per 100 acres are given in Table XX.

TABLE XX. Number of poultry per 100 acres

	Fowls	Ducks	Geese	Turkeys	Total
Group A 1	215	9·3	0·5	0·2	225
„ A 2	128	7·6	0·5	0·8	137
„ A 3	61	3·4	0·3	0·5	65
Groups A 1–A 3	114	6·4	0·4	0·6	121
Group B 1	400	11·7	0·2	0·6	413
„ B 2	146	11·1	0·5	0·7	159
„ B 3	114	12·7	0·4	0·4	128
Groups B 1–B 3	159	9·9	0·4	0·6	170

The table shows that all the holdings carry a high complement of poultry to the 100 acres, a fact which will be better realised by comparing the figures with the official estimates of the number of birds per 100 acres in the county as a whole[1]. The table also shows that the number of fowls per 100 acres in the lowlands is one and a

[1] Vide *Agricultural Statistics*, 1921, vol. LVI, part I, Table VII.

half times the corresponding number in the highlands. The larger number kept in the lowlands is partly to be explained by the need of poultry for a more even climate and for fairly dry land, while greater proximity to markets is also undoubtedly a factor.

Although the actual number of ducks per 100 acres is quite considerable, they were kept on only 31 per cent. of the highland holdings and on 41 per cent. of the lowland holdings. The numbers of both geese and turkeys per 100 acres is insignificant, geese being kept on 14 per cent., and turkeys on 18 per cent. of the holdings.

(f) *Summary*. In order to summarise the survey information on the stocking of the holdings, it is convenient to express the various types of stock in terms of a common unit. No method entirely satisfactory has so far been evolved, and it is very doubtful whether any scale which can be universally applied will ever be found. However, for the present purpose, it is perfectly safe to adopt any of the common denominators which have been used by other investigators. But it must be understood that the figures so obtained are strictly limited to their interpretation of the relative positions of the holdings in the present survey, and in no case are they meant to be compared with similar data from other districts or from other countries. With this reservation Table XXI has been prepared to show the relative stock carried on each of the six groups of holdings in this survey[1].

[1] The scale adopted is the one used by the U.S.A. Federal Department, and the units are as follows:

1	Horse, cow, or steer	1 unit
2	Young stock, horses and cattle average	1 ,,
7	Sheep	1 ,,
14	Lambs	1 ,,
10	Pigs	1 ,,
5	Hogs (pigs 200 lb. and upwards)	1 ,,
100	Fowls	1 ,,

TABLE XXI. Live-stock carried in "animal units" per 100 acres

	Cattle	Horses	Sheep	Pigs	Poultry	Total
Group A 1	38·1	4·3	3·2	2·3	2·3	50·2
„ A 2	25·1	5·3	4·8	1·4	1·4	38·0
„ A 3	15·4	3·3	9·8	0·7	0·7	29·9
Groups A 1–A 3	22·4	4·5	6·2	1·2	1·2	35·5
Group B 1	39·9	5·8	0·0	2·3	4·1	52·1
„ B 2	38·9	5·9	2·0	2·2	1·6	50·6
„ B 3	33·4	5·6	2·7	1·1	1·3	44·1
Groups B 1–B 3	37·2	5·7	2·0	1·9	1·7	48·5

The chief characteristics of the stocking of the holdings are brought out very clearly in this table. In the first place, the column giving the total number of "animal units" per 100 acres shows the higher stock-carrying capacity of the smaller holdings, and it also shows the superiority of the lowlands over the highlands. In the second place, it will be seen that this is true of each class of stock, except horses and sheep, and the reasons for the deviations in these cases have already been given in the descriptions of the various systems of management. The third point established by the table is the relative importance of the various classes of stock. Cattle are easily the most important, and account for over 70 per cent. of the "annual units" of all groups. Horses come second in all groups, except in the third highland group, which is singular in that the sheep there, representing 18 per cent. of the units, are of more importance than horses. Lastly the distribution of "animal equivalents" between pigs and poultry is seen to be varied for the different groups, which is probably due to the adaptability of these classes of stock to all types of holdings.

4. EMPLOYMENT

One of the chief social economic arguments in favour of a widely established system of small holdings is that they increase the rural population. This they are supposed to do by providing employment for a far larger number of people to the acre than the large farms. Although there

TABLE XXII. Gross number of persons employed

| | No. of holdings | Members of family | | | | Hired persons | | | | |
		Occupiers	Wives	Male relations; sons, brothers, etc.	Female relations; daughters, sisters, etc.	School children	Men	Women (maids)	Boys	Girls	Casual labour
Group A 1	19	19	16	3	3	5	0	0	2	1	0
„ A 2	64	64	53	18	19	14	3	1	8	0	16
„ A 3	17	17	13	10	10	0	2	1	4	0	3
Groups A 1–A 3	100	100	82	31	32	19	5	2	14	1	19
Group B 1	27	27	24	3	6	5	1	0	2	1	2
„ B 2	105	105	92	16	25	8	9	6	16	0	18
„ B 3	30	30	22	15	19	7	8	8	7	0	7
Groups B 1–B 3	162	162	138	34	50	20	18	14	25	1	27

can be little doubt of the general truth of this assertion, nevertheless, no accurate information exists as to the relative employment provided by the various agricultural units, since the information available (as in the "Census of Production") concerns itself only with the "density" of labour, and no distinction is drawn between full-time and part-time employment[1]. The survey information on

[1] See Ashby, *op. cit.* pp. 152–153.

this point is therefore of peculiar value inasmuch as it purports to give accurate information as to the amount of labour employed on 262 small holdings. The simple data is given in detail in Table XXII.

The comparative unimportance of hired labour is at once realised by a study of these figures of the total number of persons employed. In almost every one of the few cases where permanent labour was employed, it filled a gap in the family unit. It may be said, therefore, that all the holdings are worked by the occupier and a female help (usually his wife), assisted by other members of the family residing on the holding.

On each of the 262 small holdings one man, usually the occupier, was fully employed on the holding. Similarly, on every holding one woman, usually the wife, was also fully employed. The importance of the wife in the conduct of the small holding cannot easily be overestimated. In addition to her rôle of housewife she is in complete charge of the dairy and poultry, and takes her share of the milking, and usually of the feeding of the stock, especially of the cattle and pigs. In the busy seasons she also works in the open fields, assisting with the harvest, planting and lifting potatoes, weeding, and gathering stones, whilst she is almost entirely responsible for what little attention is paid to the garden. The children are also taught from a very early age to take an active part in the lighter work of the holding when not in actual attendance at the schools. This continual toiling of the smallholder, his wife, and his family is possibly the most serious aspect of the small holding problem, since there is reason to fear that in the struggle for a bare existence the instinct as well as the opportunity for real home-making is too often lost, and the opportunities for leisure reduced to a minimum. Such considerations, particularly that of the ratio of leisure to work, are undoubtedly "fundamental measures of the standard of living of the farm family."[1]

The other members of the family shown in Table XXII can be divided into two groups according as to whether they are fully or only partly employed on the holdings. In both groups all degrees of family relationship are found, from sons and daughters to brothers-in-law and sisters-in-law. An important characteristic of these small holdings is the way in which all available potential labour is exploited. Thus any relations employed in other occupations, but residing on the holdings, will almost certainly take some active part in the work. It may be only at busy seasons such as harvest time, or it may be in more regular employment every morning and every evening. Although it is not possible, in the absence of records, to get information of quantitative accuracy on this point, nevertheless sufficient information was obtained during the survey to make it possible to weight all these cases by a very close approximation to the actual period of time each worker was employed on the holdings. The necessary adjustment has been made in arriving at the figures shown in the next table, which gives the numbers of fully employed persons per 100 acres for the various groups, a column being added to show the same result in terms of "men equivalents" per 100 acres.

According to this table the number of fully employed persons (both males and females) per 100 acres is seen to decrease with the increase in the size of the holding, it is also considerably higher for the lowland than for the highland groups. On the smallest type of holding included

---

[1] See "Farmers' Incomes and Standards of Living" in *Journal of Farm Economics*, January 1925.

in the survey—lowland holdings under 25 acres in extent—
the total number of fully employed persons per 100 acres
expressed in terms of "men equivalents" is 10·8, being
about one person for every 9 acres. On the other hand,
the "density" of labour is considerably less on the largest
holdings, where, for example, on the highland holdings of
over 60 acres the total number of "men equivalents" per

TABLE XXIII. Number of persons fully employed
per 100 acres

	Men	Women and children	Total in men equivalents*
Group A 1	3·6	5·4	6·3
,, A 2	2·9	3·2	5·6
,, A 3	2·0	1·6	3·2
Groups A 1–A 3	2·7	2·9	4·9
Group B 1	5·4	6·1	10·8
,, B 2	3·4	3·4	6·3
,, B 3	3·3	2·8	5·4
Groups B 1–B 3	3·5	3·5	6·4

* The conversion scale used in obtaining these figures was:
1 man employed throughout the year ...   1 "man equivalent"
1 boy   ,,   ,,   0·5   ,,
1 housewife ,,   ,,   0·8   ,,
1 other female labour   ,,   0·6   ,,
School children   ,,   0·3   ,,

100 acres is only 3·2, which equals about one person to
every 31 acres. These figures, therefore, supply ample corroboration of the general opinion that the smaller holdings
create more employment than the larger farms. They do
not, however, supply any criterion of the relative efficiency
of labour in the various groups. In the next section data
of the wages of labour on these small holdings will be given,
which must be taken as a supplement to this discussion,

since the employment of a large number of people to the acre is only an advantage in so far as the remuneration they receive for their labour makes possible a satisfactory standard of living.

5. General Equipment of Holdings

The last point on which the survey data gives information is the general equipment of the holdings in buildings, machinery, and other subsidiary requirements. The farmsteads of the county are scattered over its surface, and are situated in isolated, and, particularly in the highlands, in very remote positions. This is largely a matter of historical development, and is to be explained by the "comparative modernity of most Welsh villages."[1] It is difficult to generalise as to the conditions of the homesteads, since there is so much variation from the old-fashioned and inconveniently planned holdings which are all too general in the highlands, to the more modern and convenient holdings of the valleys. On most of the holdings, however, there is no settled plan in the general arrangement of the fold and the outbuildings.

The dwelling-houses generally consist of two kitchens, often a parlour, and two or three bedrooms, whilst the dairy is almost invariably found in the house. On most of the holdings the usual equipment of outbuildings consists of a cow byre, horse stable, piggery, barn, hay shed, and cart house. The relative position in this respect of the various groups can be seen from the next table, which gives the percentage number of holdings in possession of the various types of outhouses.

It will be seen that every holding has its cow shed, many of these are, however, very inadequate, the most prevalent

---

[1] C. 8221 (1896), *op. cit.* p. 690.

TABLE XXIV. Percentage number of holdings with various outhouses

	Cow byres	Horse stables	Pig sties	Calf pens	Cart houses	Implement sheds	Barns	Hay sheds
	%	%	%	%	%	%	%	%
Group A 1	100	84	90	16	84	11	89	47
,, A 2	100	100	89	27	98	20	97	66
,, A 3	100	94	94	24	94	35	88	71
Group B 1	100	93	96	30	93	26	59	70
,, B 2	100	98	100	31	96	28	78	72
,, B 3	100	100	100	37	100	33	83	77

faults being insufficient light and ventilation, cows tied in two rows with only a narrow passage between, poor flooring usually of cobbles, and the presence of the overhead loft for the storage of straw and hay. The accommodation for calves and young cattle is very limited in all groups, and very often they are housed in unsuitable sheds of the lean-to type, or huddled in cramped spaces at the end of the cow shed.

Stables are found on the majority of holdings, though in many cases they are badly constructed, and share the drawbacks already mentioned as characterising the cow sheds. On 40 per cent. of the holdings the stables were equipped with loose boxes.

Most holdings have also their pig sties, but many of these are small, and so badly built that it is very difficult to keep them even moderately clean.

Cart houses are common, practically every holding possessing one of some description, while in addition implement sheds were found on about 20 per cent. of the holdings. It will be seen that hay sheds are popular in all groups. They are of the Dutch-barn type and usually capable of storing all the hay and corn crops of the holdings. Their introduction has proved a real boon both in reducing labour and as a means of coping with crops in fickle harvest weather.

There is a marked absence of effective accommodation for poultry, which are often housed in one of the other farm buildings, the cart houses being favourite roosting places. The management of poultry has so much to recommend itself to the smallholder, that the desirability of possessing suitable poultry houses is obvious.

Another serious defect in the equipment of the farmstead is the almost entire absence of any adequate accommodation for farmyard manure. Very often cow sheds and piggeries drain into the open yard, while a stream flows past the badly kept manure heap.

Practically all the holdings possess gardens, although the attention which they receive is often scant. This is also true of the few orchards that were seen. Here, again, the smallholder fails to take full advantage of a source of profit which is peculiarly suited to his small-scale economy. A similar criticism can be extended to include his interest in other side lines such, for example, as bee keeping, which was almost entirely ignored on the holdings visited.

Although generally the holdings are fairly compact, there still exists considerable intermixture of land which could easily be remedied. A much more serious feature is the apportionment of the land of any one holding into fields, since the big defect of a bad arrangement of too many fields is common[1]. This results in three important draw-

---

[1] The average number and the average size of fields per holding for the various groups were as follows:

	Average no. of fields per holding	Average area per field		Average no. of fields per holding	Average area per field
Group A 1	9	2·5 acres	Group B 1	4	4·6 acres
,, A 2	13	3·1 ,,	,, B 2	10	3·6 ,,
,, A 3	14	6·6 ,,	,, B 3	13	4·7 ,,

backs. First, it hinders the economic use of labour. Second, it increases the smallholder's expense in the up-keep of hedges, which for him is at best high, since he has to cope with the adverse ratio of a comparatively large boundary and a small area. Third, it results in the withdrawal of a considerable area of land from active cultivation, and thus supplies a possible objection to an extended policy of small holdings. Nevertheless, the smallest average area of $2\frac{1}{2}$ acres per field (which the table shows to obtain) cannot be regarded as an inconvenient unit for the small farmer, who prefers small fields, affording as they do a better means for the control of stock and crops.

The equipment of the holdings in implements and machinery still remains to be described. The problem of machinery presents difficulties to the smallholder which are similar to those he has to face with his horse labour. There are many machines which he needs at some period or another, but if he possesses them, they will be idle for the greater part of the year. Co-operation in the use of machinery is extraordinarily liable to lead to friction in practice. Nevertheless, ample evidence was found of the existence of spontaneous co-operation, particularly in the use of harvesting machinery, and certain barn machinery such as threshing boxes. Very often this co-operation exists between the smallholder and his neighbour on the large farm.

Table XXV gives the numbers of the various types of machines and implements found per 100 acres, as well as the percentage of the holdings in each group on which they were kept.

The number of vehicles per 100 acres is seen to fall with the rise in the size of the holding for both highland and lowland groups. Practically every holding has its cart or "gambo"; the "gambo" or "longbody" is very common in the county and is well suited for work in hilly country.

There are comparatively few cultivation implements found on the smallest holdings, especially in the lowlands. On most of the other holdings the usual equipment includes a plough, harrow, horse hoe, and chain harrow or roller.

Harvesting machines are also naturally fewer on the smaller holdings. The most usual quota per holding consists of a mowing machine, a tedder, and a horse rake.

The barn machine which seems indispensable to all holdings is the chaff cutter, while the percentage of holdings possessing threshing and winnowing machines is considerably higher for the highlands than for the lowlands.

The interesting feature of the figures given for the dairy utensils is the very low percentage of holdings possessing butter makers. When it is remembered that on the majority of holdings butter is made for sale, it will be realised how primitive must be the process by which most of it is prepared.

The simple horse gear is the power generator most generally used, although a considerable number of holdings in all groups possess oil or petrol engines, while water wheels were in use on 19 of the holdings.

Unfortunately the survey data for harness and small implements equipment are not sufficiently exhaustive for tabular presentation. However, most holdings possess the necessary complement of such harness and tools as are indispensable for the proper conduct of the farms.

TABLE XXV. Number of implements and machines per 100 acres, and percentage of holdings with same

	Group A 1		Group A 2		Group A 3		Group B 1		Group B 2		Group B 3	
	No. of machines per 100 acres	% of holdings with machines	No. of machines per 100 acres	% of holdings with machines	No. of machines per 100 acres	% of holdings with machines	No. of machines per 100 acres	% of holdings with machines	No. of machines per 100 acres	% of holdings with machines	No. of machines per 100 acres	% of holdings with machines
Vehicles												
Carts	3.6	84	2.6	100	1.2	100	4.5	89	2.8	100	2.0	100
Gambos	2.3	52	2.2	92	1.0	88	2.8	59	2.3	87	1.8	100
Traps	1.8	42	1.9	78	0.8	71	2.4	48	1.7	64	0.9	53
Milk floats	0.0	0	0.0	0	0.0	0	0.4	7	0.1	5	0.2	10
Spring gambos	0.7	16	0.1	5	0.1	6	1.3	26	0.6	23	0.9	53
Cultivating implements												
Ploughs												
Single-furrow	3.4	79	2.5	100	1.2	100	3.2	63	2.5	92	2.2	100
Double-furrow	0.0	0	0.3	14	0.5	41	0.0	0	0.2	6	0.1	7
Harrows												
Zig-zag	3.2	74	2.4	100	1.0	94	2.4	48	2.2	82	1.7	100
Spring tooth	0.2	5	0.8	31	0.5	41	0.0	0	0.4	16	0.8	50
Chain	0.5	11	1.4	56	0.7	65	2.6	52	2.1	78	1.3	77
Cultivators	0.7	16	1.0	41	0.5	47	0.4	7	0.6	22	0.6	33
Horse hoes	0.5	11	1.1	45	0.7	65	0.4	7	1.0	38	0.8	50
Rollers	0.7	16	1.4	56	0.8	76	0.9	19	1.3	51	1.2	73

Drills												
Small seed ...	0·0	0	0·3	14	0·3	29	0·0	0	0·1	5	0·1	7
Corn ...	0·0	0	0·1	5	0·1	6	0·0	0	0·1	3	0·6	7
Manure spreaders ...	0·0	0	0·0	0	0·0	0	0·0	0	0·0	0	0·3	20
Harvesting machinery												
Self-binder ...	0·0	0	0·2	8	0·1	12	0·0	0	0·1	4	0·3	20
Reaping machine ...	1·8	42	0·2	9	0·1	12	0·0	0	0·0	0	0·1	3
Mowing machine ...	0·0	0	2·4	98	0·9	82	2·4	48	2·4	90	1·8	100
Side-delivery rake ...	0·0	0	0·0	0	0·0	0	0·0	0	0·5	19	0·1	3
Swath turner ...	0·0	0	0·0	2	0·0	0	0·6	11	0·3	10	0·4	23
Hay loader ...	0·0	0	0·0	0	0·0	0	0·0	0	0·2	7	0·1	10
Haymakers and tedder	1·1	26	1·0	42	0·5	47	1·3	26	0·9	35	1·1	67
Horse rake ...	1·6	89	1·5	64	0·8	76	2·4	48	1·9	71	1·6	97
Elevator (in hay shed)	0·0	0	0·2	6	0·0	0	0·2	4	0·9	32	0·9	53
Barn machinery												
Threshing machine ...	1·1	32	2·0	81	0·9	82	0·2	4	1·0	36	0·9	53
Winnowing machine ...	1·6	89	1·8	75	0·9	82	0·4	7	0·9	34	0·9	53
Grinding mill ...	0·2	5	0·2	9	0·2	18	0·4	7	0·2	7	0·4	27
Chaff cutter ...	3·4	79	2·4	100	1·0	88	4·6	93	2·6	97	1·6	97
Pulper ...	2·0	47	1·4	58	0·8	71	1·7	33	1·5	58	1·2	73
Cake crusher ...	0·2	5	0·1	3	0·1	6	0·2	4	0·2	9	0·3	20
Dairy utensils												
Separator ...	3·4	79	1·9	78	0·8	76	3·5	70	2·2	84	1·4	83
Steel churns ...	0·0	0	0·0	0	0·0	0	1·9	22	1·6	30	2·7	53
Butter churns ...	4·3	100	2·4	100	1·0	94	4·6	89	2·6	98	1·6	93
Butter makers ...	0·2	5	0·3	14	0·2	18	0·4	7	0·7	26	0·3	20
Cheese press ...	2·7	63	1·7	70	0·8	77	2·8	56	1·7	68	1·1	67
Power machinery												
Horse gear ...	1·1	32	1·5	64	0·5	47	0·7	15	1·2	46	0·5	30
Water wheels ...	0·2	5	0·2	6	0·3	24	0·0	0	0·2	6	0·3	17
Oil and petrol engines	0·5	11	0·5	20	0·2	18	0·9	19	0·6	22	0·7	40

C. ANALYSIS OF 93 FINANCIAL ACCOUNTS

1. CLASSIFICATION

The information set out in the first part of this section represents that which was obtained by the survey method of research into agricultural economic phenomena. It will have been observed how this method supplies valuable information on such important points as systems of husbandry, equipment of holdings, labour complement, etc. In other words, it represents that information which the average farmer, of ordinary business acumen, can give in the course of an ordinary conversation or interview. But, in the absence of some record or account, it is beyond the ability of the most intelligent of farmers to give information which will be sufficiently accurate to form a basis for the estimation, either of the net output of farms, or of the standard of living of those engaged in the enterprise. Consequently, in order to supplement the survey information, an attempt was made to secure the further services of the more responsive smallholders met with during the survey, who were asked to co-operate by keeping simple financial accounts of their undertakings for a period of one year. The data obtained in this manner form the raw material of the results analysed in the following pages.

Altogether 120 financial accounts were received, but after careful winnowing it has been possible to make use of 93 only, the remaining 27 having to be disregarded on account of their lack of completeness in one respect or another. A larger number would of course have been a decided advantage, though it is believed that these 93 holdings are sufficiently representative to ensure that an analysis of their financial accounts supplies a fair indication of the real economic position of the general body of Carmarthenshire smallholders.

In classifying the 93 holdings from which financial accounts were received, it has not been possible, unfortunately, to retain exactly the same division as was used in the analysis of the large survey. The division into highland and lowland holdings has been retained, but a slight modification of the acreage grouping has had to be adopted. This has been made necessary because of the unequal response obtained from the several groups used in the larger survey. The highland group under 30 acres in extent has had to be omitted entirely, since the number of accounts obtained for this group was too meagre to justify analysis. On the other hand, it has been considered necessary to include as a new group those lowland holdings on which milk-selling is practised. The justification for this will be found later in the many points of difference which this group presents, making it very desirable to treat it separately. The detailed classification of these 93 small holdings is shown in Table XXVI.

It will be seen that of the 64 lowland holdings included, 13 are in the new milk-selling group. The other 51 lowland holdings are divided into acreage groups as follows: 13 under 25 acres, 24 between 25 acres and 40 acres, and 14 over 40 acres. There are 29 highland holdings, 11 of which are under 40 acres, 10 between 40 and 60 acres, and 8 over 60 acres. The average rentals per holding and per acre are also given in the table. Here again, as in the classification of the large survey, it will be noticed that there is a fair correlation of type between highland and lowland groups when quality as well as quantity of land is taken into account.

It is necessary here to say a word about the scheme

adopted in the following discussion of these financial accounts. The first part of the treatment is a straight-forward analysis of the data of the financial accounts themselves, under the headings of gross sales and money expenses, together with the rough approximation to the

TABLE XXVI. Classification of 93 small holdings keeping financial accounts

	No. of holdings in group	Total acreage	Average size of holding (acres)	Average rental per holding			Average rental per acre		
				£	s.	d.	£	s.	d.
A. *Highland holdings*									
(1) Under 40 acres	11	383	34·8	27	12	9		15	11
(2) 40–60 acres	10	486	48·6	36	18	0		15	2
(3) Over 60 acres	8	713	89·0	48	5	0		10	10
Average	29	1582	54·6	38	1	1		13	11
B. *Mixed lowland holdings*									
(1) Under 25 acres	13	291	22·3	27	15	5	1	4	11
(2) 25–40 acres	24	777	32·4	41	15	10	1	5	9
(3) Over 40 acres	14	643	45·9	56	14	3	1	4	9
Average	51	1711	33·6	43	4	9	1	5	2
C. *Milk-selling lowland holdings*	13	502	38·6	72	12	4	1	11	8

net returns obtained by considering these factors only. The second part of the discussion, on the other hand, is more elaborate. Estimates are introduced by which the more exact data of the financial accounts have to be supplemented before a complete conception can be obtained of both the net output of the small holdings, and of the standard of living of the smallholders.

2. GROSS SALES OR MONEY RECEIPTS

The financial accounts furnished a detailed record of all the sales from the 93 small holdings for the period of one year. At the outset, it is important not to confuse the value of these sales with the value of the total production of the holdings. The sales only comprise that part of the gross production which is represented by money receipts. To obtain the true value of the gross production other factors, such as the value of the foodstuffs consumed off the holdings by the family, must be added. The value of the sales can, therefore, be taken only as a rough indication of the value of the gross output of the holdings.

By classifying the data of the financial accounts it is possible to give an analysis of the sales for the various branches of the farm. Such an analysis is given in detail in Table XXVII.

The table illustrates very clearly the fall in the value of the sales per acre with the increase in the size of the holdings, and with the increase in the altitude. Taking first the movement with the size of the holding, the total sales are seen to drop in the highlands from £5. 7s. 7d. per acre in the first group to £3. 8s. 1d. per acre in the third group. Similarly, in the lowlands, there is a drop from the first to the third group in this case of 11s. 1d. For the highland groups this fall in sales with rise in acreage is seen to be uniform for all the branches with the exception of sheep, which shows a higher sale per acre on the larger holdings. The tendency is almost equally marked in the lowland holdings, although there is an actual rise here in the sales of cattle and dairy produce with the increase in acreage, which is probably due to the fact that comparatively more mature stock are sold off

TABLE XXVII. Gross sales per acre, and their percentage distribution

	Highland holdings				Lowland holdings				
					Mixed holdings				Milk-selling holdings
	Under 40 acres	40–60 acres	Over 60 acres	Average	Under 25 acres	25–40 acres	Over 40 acres	Average	
	£ s. d.	£ s. d.	£ s. d.	£ s. d.	£ s. d.	£ s. d.	£ s. d.	£ s. d.	£ s. d.
Cattle ...	1 15 2 32·70 %	1 12 5 31·14 %	0 14 5 21·17 %	1 5 0 28·09 %	1 19 2 25·31 %	2 0 3 26·41 %	2 3 6 30·28 %	2 1 4 27·63 %	2 3 11 19·84 %
Dairy produce	1 4 3 22·56 %	1 2 10 21·93 %	0 13 0 19·09 %	0 18 8 22·92 %	2 1 4 26·71 %	2 3 2 28·32 %	2 4 10 31·21 %	2 3 5 29·03 %	6 14 0 60·57 %
Horses ...	0 2 6 2·32 %	0 2 5 2·33 %	0 1 5 2·08 %	0 2 0 2·00 %	0 0 6 0·32 %	0 4 10 3·16 %	0 2 8 1·85 %	0 3 4 2·22 %	0 3 1 1·39 %
Sheep ...	0 10 10 10·07 %	0 17 2 16·49 %	1 0 8 30·35 %	0 17 2 19·36 %	0 10 10 7·01 %	0 10 2 6·66 %	0 12 1 8·41 %	0 11 0 7·35 %	0 6 4 2·86 %
Pigs ...	0 14 8 13·62 %	0 12 2 11·69 %	0 10 10 15·92 %	0 12 2 13·02 %	1 12 9 21·16 %	1 8 5 18·63 %	1 0 10 14·50 %	1 6 4 17·61 %	0 12 3 5·54 %
Poultry ...	0 19 1 17·72 %	0 17 1 16·42 %	0 7 3 10·66 %	0 13 2 14·05 %	1 10 1 19·45 %	1 3 10 15·68 %	0 19 8 13·69 %	1 3 4 15·60 %	1 1 6 9·72 %
Other receipts	0 1 1 1·01 %	0 0 0 0·00 %	0 0 6 0·73 %	0 0 6 0·56 %	0 0 1 0·04 %	0 1 9 1·14 %	0 0 1 0·06 %	0 0 10 0·56 %	0 0 2 0·08 %
Total ...	5 7 7 100·00 %	5 4 1 100·00 %	3 8 1 100·00 %	4 8 8 100·00 %	7 14 9 100·00 %	7 12 5 100·00 %	7 3 8 100·00 %	7 9 7 100·00 %	11 1 3 100·00 %

the larger holdings. Secondly, the adverse movement of the sales with the altitude is seen from the fact that the average total sales per acre is only £4. 8s. 8d. in the highlands, while the corresponding figure for the lowlands is £7. 9s. 7d. Moreover, the lowlands show a higher sale per acre for each of the branches of the farm with the exception of sheep, while the far higher sales of dairy produce in the milk-selling holdings give this group the highest total sales per acre.

The mixed nature of the production of the holdings is well illustrated in the table by the figures giving the average sales for all groups. The sales from each of the branches of the farm, with the exception of horses and crops, are well represented in the percentage figures, thus showing the importance of each in the economy of the holdings. For example, in the highlands over 13 per cent. of the total sales are made up of sales from cattle, from dairy produce, from sheep, from pigs, and from poultry respectively. Similarly, for the lowlands, with the exception of sheep, each of these branches accounts for over 15 per cent. of the total sales. In the milk-selling holdings, however, the fact that 60 per cent. of the total sales are sales of dairy produce makes the sales from the remaining branches relatively unimportant. Further details will now be given of the sales from each branch of the farm, taken in the order given in Table XXVII.

(a) *Cattle and Dairy produce.* In the first place the predominant importance of cattle is shown by the fact that sales of cattle and dairy produce together make up 50 per cent. of the total sales of most of the groups. In the milk-selling group dairy produce alone accounts for over 60 per cent. of all the sales. The one exception is the third highland group where the sales from sheep form 30 per cent. of the total sales, thus lowering the percentage sales from cattle and dairy produce to 40. The details of these sales will now be given in two separate tables. The first table (Table XXVIII) shows the sales of stock per acre under the headings of cows, one to two year old cattle, and calves.

TABLE XXVIII. Sales of cattle per acre

	Cows			One to two year old cattle			Calves			Total			Per-centage of total sales
	£	s.	d.	£	s.	d.	£	s.	d.	£	s.	d.	
Group A 1	0	15	5	0	16	7	0	3	2	1	15	2	32·70
„ A 2	0	12	9	0	17	8	0	2	0	1	12	5	31·14
„ A 3	0	6	1	0	7	1	0	1	3	0	14	5	21·17
Group B 1	1	2	0	0	10	1	0	7	1	1	19	2	25·31
„ B 2	0	17	0	0	16	10	0	6	5	2	0	3	26·41
„ B 3	0	14	10	1	5	3	0	3	5	2	3	6	30·28
Group C	0	16	8	0	15	3	0	12	0	2	3	11	19·84

The table shows that sales of cattle are a comparatively more important item on the highland holdings, where greater attention is paid to rearing. Thus the receipts from the sales of yearlings and two year old cattle are comparatively higher for the highland groups, and, conversely, the receipts from the sales of calves are higher for the milk-selling group. Unfortunately the data are not sufficiently detailed to give the exact ratio of the sales of fat stock to the sales of store cattle.

While the sale of stock is comparatively more important in the highlands, Table XXIX shows the converse to be true for the sales of dairy produce.

Both the sales per acre of dairy produce and the percentage which they form of the total sales are very much higher for the milk-selling group. This is not necessarily due to superior production, since the relative prices of butter and whole milk are also important factors. Comparing the other lowland groups with the highland groups, it is seen that the sale of butter is more than double on the latter than on the former. The sale of milk shown in groups A 1 and A 2 represents a little retailing done with villagers or neighbours. Cheese was sold on only five of the holdings.

TABLE XXIX. Sales of dairy produce per acre

	Milk			Butter			Cheese			Total			Percentage of total sales
	£	s.	d.	£	s.	d.	£	s.	d.	£	s.	d.	
Group A 1	0	0	1	1	0	2	0	4	0	1	4	3	22·56
„ A 2	0	0	10	1	1	3	0	0	9	1	2	10	21·93
„ A 3	—			0	13	0	—			0	13	0	19·09
Group B 1	—			2	1	4	—			2	1	4	26·71
„ B 2	—			2	3	2	—			2	3	2	28·32
„ B 3	—			2	4	3	0	0	7	2	4	10	31·21
Group C	6	10	6	0	3	6	—			6	14	0	60·57

(b) *Horses.* It was pointed out in the previous section that the horse economy of many of the holdings was disorganised as a result of the very adverse state of the horse market. It is not safe, therefore, to draw many conclusions from the figures given of the sales of horses for the various groups. Moreover, this is also comparatively unnecessary, since the sale of horses was restricted to 7 highland holdings and to 13 lowland holdings. The highest sale per acre recorded was 4s. 10d. in the 25–40 acre lowland group, where the sale of horses formed only 3 per cent. of the total sales.

(c) *Sheep.* Sheep are not generally associated with the small holding; nevertheless, the details of the sales of sheep shown in the next table indicate that they are by no means unimportant on the holdings under investigation.

TABLE XXX. Sales of sheep per acre

	Ewes and yearlings			Lambs			Wool			Total			Percentage of total sales
	£	s.	d.	£	s.	d.	£	s.	d.	£	s.	d.	
Group A 1	0	1	6	0	8	7	0	0	9	0	10	10	10·07
„ A 2	0	4	9	0	10	9	0	1	8	0	17	2	16·49
„ A 3	0	5	8	0	13	4	0	1	8	1	0	8	30·35
Group B 1	0	7	10	0	2	6	0	0	6	0	10	10	7·01
„ B 2	0	3	10	0	5	9	0	0	7	0	10	2	6·66
„ B 3	0	3	3	0	8	2	0	0	8	0	12	1	8·41
Group C	0	1	8	0	4	4	0	0	4	0	6	4	2·86

That they are of greater importance, first in the highlands, and, secondly, on the larger holdings, are results which would naturally be expected. Thus, for example, in the three lowland groups the receipts from sheep sales average only 7 per cent. of the total money income, but they account for over 19 per cent. of the average money income of the highland holdings, the percentage being over 30 for the highland holdings over 60 acres in extent. Again, the gross sales per acre of sheep range from 10s. 10d. in the first highland group to £1. 0s. 8d. in the third highland group. Similarly, in the lowlands, the sales per acre are higher on the larger holdings[1], they are least for the milk-selling farms where sheep form only 2·86 per cent.

[1] The unexpected high sale per acre in Group B 1 is due to the practice obtaining on one 24 acre holding included, where some 30 ewes bought in September are kept over the winter and sold with their lambs sometime in May.

of the total sales. The next point demonstrated by the table is the fact that the sale of mature stock is the more important aspect in the lowlands, while in the highlands the sale of lambs is far more important. This result is a necessary corollary of the two different systems of sheep management already described as existing in the highlands and lowlands respectively[1].

(d) *Pigs.* Pigs differ from sheep in being generally considered as adapted to the special needs of the small holding, and they form the origin of about 14 per cent. of the average total sales of all the holdings included in the survey. Considered in relation to other branches of the farm, the receipts from the sales of pigs are least important in the milk-selling holdings where they form only 5·5 per cent. of the total money income. They are most important on the mixed lowland holdings, forming over 21 per cent. of the total sales in the group of holdings under 25 acres in extent. The detailed analysis of the pig sales is given in Table XXXI, which again shows clearly the drop in sales with rise in both acreage and altitude.

TABLE XXXI. Sales of pigs per acre

	Baconers	Porkers	Weaners	Bacon	Total	Percentage of total sales
	£ s. d.	£ s. d.	£ s. d.	£ s. d.	£ s. d.	
Group A 1	0 1 9	0 7 10	0 4 4	0 0 9	0 14 8	13·62
„ A 2	0 2 10	0 4 6	0 3 5	0 1 5	0 12 2	11·69
„ A 3	0 1 2	0 5 3	0 4 5	—	0 10 10	15·92
Group B 1	0 7 10	0 17 7	0 5 1	0 2 3	1 12 9	21·16
„ B 2	0 3 10	0 17 3	0 6 8	0 0 8	1 8 5	18·63
„ B 3	—	0 14 2	0 6 4	0 0 4	1 0 10	14·50
Group C	0 1 7	0 7 2	0 3 6	—	0 12 3	5·54

[1] *Vide ante*, pp. 44, 45.

The mainstay of the pig trade is seen to be the sale of porkers and weaners. Comparatively more porkers are sold in the lowland holdings, and more weaners in the highlands. This agrees with the fact that more breeding sows are kept in comparison on the highland holdings, while the more prevalent custom in the lowlands is to buy several lots of weaners, selling them later as porkers[1]. The practice of selling bacon is not prevalent, and was restricted to 8 holdings only, where odd sides of bacon and ham were sold to neighbouring villagers.

TABLE XXXII. Sales of poultry per acre

	Fowls and chickens			Ducks			Geese			Turkeys			Eggs			Total			% of total sales
	£	s.	d.	£	s.	d.	£	s.	d.	£	s.	d.	£	s.	d.	£	s.	d.	
Group A 1	0	2	1	0	0	4	0	0	1	0	0	8	0	15	11	0	19	1	17·72
„ A 2	0	1	5	0	0	2	0	0	3	0	0	3	0	15	0	0	17	1	16·42
„ A 3	0	0	11	0	0	1	0	0	1	0	0	11	0	5	3	0	7	3	10·66
Group B 1	0	3	6	0	0	4	0	1	1	0	1	4	1	3	10	1	10	1	19·45
„ B 2	0	1	9	0	0	9	0	0	3	0	1	3	0	19	10	1	3	10	15·68
„ B 3	0	1	10	0	0	1	0	0	5	0	1	8	0	15	8	0	19	8	13·69
Group C	0	2	4	0	0	10	—			—			0	18	4	1	1	6	9·72

(e) *Poultry.* Like pigs, poultry are also recognised as being well adapted to the small holding, both as the predominant factor of the more specialised holding as well as an important branch of those small farms on which a system of mixed husbandry prevails. Table XXXII, which gives the details for this branch, shows that the drop in sales with rise in acreage and altitude applies also to poultry; it also shows the greater comparative importance of poultry on the smaller holdings.

[1] Compare *ante,* Table XVIII, p. 46.

Thus, sales of poultry make up 17·72 per cent. of the total sales in the smallest highland group, but only 10·66 per cent. in the third highland group. Similarly, in the lowlands, 19·45 per cent. of the total sales in Group B 1 are from poultry, while the corresponding figure for Group B 3 is only 13·69 per cent. The bulk of the sales is seen to consist of eggs, which form an average of over 80 per cent. of the total receipts from poultry in each group. The sale of fowls, ducks, geese, and turkeys are correspondingly unimportant. Ducks were sold from 23 holdings, geese from 9 holdings, and turkeys from 14 holdings.

(f) *Crops.* Inasmuch as the sources of over 98 per cent. of the receipts of each group have already been discussed, there is very little to say about the one source remaining. Since practically all the crops grown on the small holdings investigated are consumed on the holdings themselves, it follows that the sales from crops are practically negligible for all groups. Potatoes was the only crop sold from the three highland groups, while in the lowlands small quantities of hay, swedes, turnips, and cabbage plants were also sold.

3. MONEY EXPENSES

Just as the data of the gross sales contained in the financial accounts do not represent the real gross output, so, also, their data regarding the expenses incurred give an incomplete picture of the total expense of running the holdings. Here, again, the data available are limited to those which are represented by money transactions only; to obtain the real gross expense, therefore, other factors, such as remuneration of family labour and interest on

capital, must be added. The money expenses of the 93
small holdings of the survey are analysed in detail in
Table XXXIII, which gives the amount per acre of the
various types of expenses, together with their percentage
distribution for each of the seven groups.

In the same way as the total sales per acre were seen
to decrease with the increase in both acreage and altitude,
so also there is a general tendency for the total money
expenses, when viewed on an acreage basis, to fall with the
rise in the size of the holding, while they are much higher
for the lowland farms, being highest here again for the
milk-selling group. On the other hand, there is a marked
difference between the distribution of the sales and the
distribution of the money expenses. While the former were
observed to be distributed fairly evenly between the various
items, over 65 per cent. of the average money expenses
of all the holdings occur under the two items of rent and
purchases of feeding stuffs. Each of these items of expense will now be considered separately under the various
headings used in the table opposite.

Rent and rates together account for over 34 per cent.
of the average total expenses of all the holdings. The
importance of these two items of expense to the smallholder will, therefore, at once be realised. For the highland groups both rent and rates are seen to fall regularly
with the rise in acreage; for example, rent drops from
16s. 2d. per acre in the first group to 11s. 5d. per acre in
the third group, rates falling similarly from 4s. per acre
to 2s. 3d. per acre. There is not much variation in the rental
per acre of the three lowland groups. Both rent and rates
are considerably higher for the lowland holdings, being
highest for the milk-selling group. Nevertheless, the proportion which rent and rates together form of the total

TABLE XXXIII. Money expenses per acre, and their percentage distribution

| | Highland holdings | | | | Lowland holdings | | | | |
| | Under 40 acres | 40-60 acres | Over 60 acres | Average | Mixed holdings | | | | Milk-selling holdings |
					Under 25 acres	25-40 acres	Over 40 acres	Average	
Rent … …	£ s. d. 0 16 2 30·52 %	£ s. d. 0 15 9 28·72 %	£ s. d. 0 11 5 36·23 %	£ s. d. 0 13 7 30·87 %	£ s. d. 1 5 3 25·96 %	£ s. d. 1 6 7 28·35 %	£ s. d. 1 5 1 27·34 %	£ s. d. 1 5 3 27·01 %	£ s. d. 1 18 8 27·74 %
Rates … …	0 4 0 7·54 %	0 3 4 6·08 %	0 2 3 7·14 %	0 3 0 6·82 %	0 6 3 6·43 %	0 5 5 5·77 %	0 5 5 5·90 %	0 5 7 5·99 %	0 7 11 5·68 %
Hired labour …	0 0 0 0·00 %	0 0 0 0·00 %	0 0 0 0·00 %	0 0 0 0·00 %	0 0 1 0·08 %	0 0 2 0·18 %	0 2 1 2·27 %	0 0 10 0·90 %	0 6 1 4·36 %
Feeding stuffs …	1 3 0 43·31 %	1 2 0 40·12 %	0 10 7 33·33 %	0 17 1 38·83 %	2 2 5 43·63 %	1 12 6 34·67 %	1 15 11 39·15 %	1 15 7 38·29 %	2 7 0 33·71 %
Manures … …	0 1 3 2·34 %	0 2 1 3·80 %	0 1 7 5·02 %	0 1 11 4·36 %	0 3 1 3·17 %	0 2 1 2·22 %	0 2 8 2·91 %	0 2 6 2·68 %	0 3 0 2·15 %
Seeds … …	0 1 5 2·67 %	0 2 2 3·96 %	0 1 0 3·18 %	0 1 7 3·59 %	0 1 5 1·46 %	0 1 10 1·96 %	0 1 2 1·27 %	0 1 6 1·61 %	0 0 3 0·18 %
Purchases of livestock	0 4 6 8·41 %	0 6 1 11·09 %	0 3 0 9·54 %	0 4 4 9·85 %	0 13 8 14·05 %	0 18 7 19·82 %	0 15 1 16·44 %	0 16 5 17·62 %	1 9 6 21·16 %
Other expenses …	0 2 9 5·15 %	0 3 5 6·23 %	0 1 9 5·56 %	0 2 6 5·68 %	0 5 1 5·22 %	0 6 7 7·03 %	0 4 4 4·72 %	0 5 6 5·90 %	0 7 0 5·02 %
Total … …	2 13 1	2 14 10	1 11 7	2 4 0	4 17 3	4 13 9	4 11 9	4 13 2	6 19 5

expenses is higher for each of the highland groups, thus making these two items of expense comparatively more important to the highland smallholder.

The expense per acre incurred on hired labour is in marked contrast to that on rent and rates. It will be observed that it is practically negligible for all groups. This result is only to be expected since holdings employing hired labour were excluded as far as possible from the survey, such holdings being outside the interpretation given at the start of the type of holding to be investigated. Moreover, the few cases in the lowlands on which hired labour was employed are to be explained by the need for filling in gaps in the family unit. The remuneration of the family for its work is the real wages problem of the small holding and this will be dealt with at some length later on.

While the Carmarthenshire smallholder obtains most of his bulky feeding stuffs from his pasture and hay land, his comparatively small arable area makes it necessary for him to depend almost entirely on purchases for his supply of the more concentrated foods. The result is seen in the fact that the expense incurred in the purchase of feeding stuffs is even more important than the combined expense of rent and rates. For example, over 37 per cent. of the average total money expenses of all the holdings occurs under this item. This percentage is least for the milk-selling group, while it is slightly lower for the mixed holdings of the lowlands than for the highland holdings. The actual expense per acre, however, is more than doubled for the lowlands, where the highest is £2. 7s. 0d. per acre for the milk-selling holdings. For both highland and lowland groups, a fall in the amount of the feeding stuffs bill obtains with the increase in acreage. The expense per acre on the various types of feeding stuffs was as follows:

	Group A 1			Group A 2			Group A 3			Group B 1			Group B 2			Group B 3			Group C		
	£	s.	d.	£	s.	d.	£	s.	d.	£	s.	d.	£	s.	d.	£	s.	d.	£	s.	d.
Barley meal	0	7	0	0	9	0	0	5	3	0	16	1		10	3	0	10	7	0	6	1
Bran	0	2	4	0	2	1	0	0	3	0	4	2	0	3	8	0	2	6	0	5	3
Maize	0	9	7	0	6	0	0	3	2	0	12	10	0	8	10	0	10	10	0	8	10
Maize meal	0	0	11	0	0	6	0	0	6	0	1	8	0	2	0	0	0	4	0	7	4
Sharps	0	0	2	0	0	0	0	0	2	0	1	5	0	1	2	0	0	8	0	1	8
Cakes	0	2	5	0	1	10	0	1	0	0	1	9	0	4	0	0	5	2	0	12	0
Other feeding stuffs	0	0	7	0	2	7	0	0	3	0	4	6	0	2	7	0	5	10	0	5	10
Total	1	3	0	1	2	0	0	10	7	2	2	5	1	12	6	1	15	11	2	7	0

It will be seen that, for all groups, the purchases of barley meal, bran, and maize account for the bulk of the feeding stuffs bill; this shows that the pig economy is mostly responsible for this item of expense. The highest figure for the purchase of the more concentrated foods, such as cake, is shown for the milk-selling holdings. It is also relatively more important in the lowland than in the highland holdings, although it is also considerable for the smallest highland group.

There is very little variation from group to group in the expense of buying artificial manures, although the actual expense per acre is slightly more for the lowland holdings. This expense is comparatively small for all groups, the average being only 2s. 4d. per acre. The chief artificial manure bought is basic slag which is freely used on the pasture land, superphosphate coming next in importance. The relative importance of the other manures is seen from the following table which gives the total amount expended on all the holdings, together with the percentage distribution of this expense between the various types of fertilisers.

The amount of arable land undoubtedly influences the quantity and quality of the manures purchased, but it has even more effect on the purchases of seeds. The comparatively small outlay on seeds—an average of 1s. 4d. per acre for all holdings—is, therefore, easily explained by the very small area of arable land obtaining. The highest expense incurred in the purchase of seeds was 2s. 2d. an

	Value of manure purchased			Percentage of total manure bill
	£	s.	d.	
Basic slag	221	7	7	60·8
Superphosphate	106	1	10	29·1
Sulphate of ammonia ...	5	14	6	1·6
Nitrate of soda	1	6	0	0·4
Kainit	2	14	0	0·6
Sutton's Special Manure ...	4	18	6	1·4
Bone manures	11	11	0	3·3
Lime	10	8	1	2·8
Total	£364	1	6	100·0

acre for the second group of highland holdings. It is not possible from the data available to give in detail the gross expenses for the various types of seeds, but oats, barley, clover and grass seeds make up the bulk of the purchases.

Next to feeding stuffs and rent the most considerable item of expense for all groups is the purchase of live stock. The actual expense per acre under this head is, however, nearly four times as large in the lowlands as in the highlands. This has its influence on the percentage which purchases of live stock form of the total expenses—under 10 per cent. in the highlands, but over 17 per cent. in the lowlands, while for the milk-selling group it is 21·16 per cent. This is really a reflection of an important difference in the respective systems of farming, and in order to illustrate it further the following table gives the amounts per acre spent in buying the various types of live stock, first, for the highland holdings, secondly, for the mixed lowland holdings, and thirdly, for the milk-selling group.

Purchases of live stock per acre

	Highland holdings			Mixed lowland holdings			Milk-selling holdings		
	£	*s.*	*d.*	£	*s.*	*d.*	£	*s.*	*d.*
Cattle ...	0	0	10	0	4	9	1	0	5
Calves ...	0	0	3	0	1	6	0	0	10
Horses ...	0	0	8	0	2	2	0	3	3
Sheep ...	0	1	1	0	2	7	0	0	8
Pigs ...	0	1	6	0	5	4	0	4	4
Poultry ...	0	0	0	0	0	1	0	0	0
Total ...	0	4	4	0	16	5	1	9	6

Taking, first, the purchases of cattle, it will be seen that it is practically negligible in the highlands; in the mixed lowland holdings, on the other hand, it forms over 38 per cent. of the total purchases of stock, and in the milk-selling group it is about two-thirds of the total or approximately £1 an acre. This is due to the practice on the lowlands of buying in from the highlands store cattle to be fattened. The much higher purchases of cattle in the milk-selling group is due to the prevalent custom of buying in-calf heifers and cows for replenishing the milch herd. In the same manner the lowland practice of, first, purchasing sheep and fattening rather than keeping breeding ewes, and, second, as regards pigs, of buying weaners to be sold as porkers, are both reflected in the higher expense incurred in the purchases of sheep and pigs.

Under "other expenses," shown in the last row of Table XXXIII, are included such items as tradesmen's

bills, veterinary fees, service fees, licences, purchases of
new machinery, etc. Unfortunately, it is not possible to
give a detailed analysis of these miscellaneous expenses.
With the exception of purchases of machinery[1], and
veterinary fees, they may be regarded as being more or
less a permanent annual charge on all holdings.

4. BALANCE OF MONEY RECEIPTS AND MONEY EXPENSES

It has been seen how the amounts per acre of both the
money receipts and the money expenses fall with the increase in the size of the holding, as well as with the increase
in the altitude. A similar tendency in their resultant
balance is also to be observed, and this is shown in the
next table, which gives the balance per acre of expenses
and receipts per acre and per holding.

This tendency is quite regular for the highland holdings
where there is a consecutive fall in the balance per acre
of 5s. 3d. and 12s. 8d. between the three groups. In the
lowland holdings, however, the balance per acre is actually
higher for the second than for the first group—a fact
explained by the very high ratio of expenses to sales
obtaining for this first group. The highest balance per acre
is shown for the milk-selling group, while the average
balance per acre is higher by more than 11s. for the mixed
holdings of the lowlands than it is for the highland
holdings.

---

[1] The expense of purchasing machinery and other equipment was as
follows:

			s.	d.	
Group A 1	...	...	0	0	per acre
,, A 2	...	...	0	9	,,
,, A 3	...	...	0	0	,,
Group B 1	...	...	1	7	,,
,, B 2	...	...	3	4	,,
,, B 3	...	...	1	2	,,
Group C	...	...	3	7	,,

The balance per holding which is also given in Table XXXIV has been inserted as a rough indication of the net money income of the small holdings. It has already been stressed that, for the small holdings investigated, the "unit

TABLE XXXIV. Balance of money receipts and money expenses (1) per acre, (2) per holding

	Highland holdings											
	Under 40 acres			40–60 acres			Over 60 acres			Average		
	£	s.	d.	£	s.	d.	£	s.	d.	£	s.	d.
Money receipts												
Per acre ...	5	7	7	5	4	1	3	8	1	4	8	8
Per holding ...	186	17	8	253	4	6	303	6	1	245	7	3
Money expenses												
Per acre ...	2	13	1	2	14	10	1	11	6	2	4	0
Per holding ...	93	9	8	137	5	6	155	1	3	120	0	9
Balance												
Per acre ...	2	14	6	2	9	3	1	16	7	2	4	8
Per holding ...	93	8	0	115	19	0	148	4	10	125	6	6

	Lowland holdings														
	Mixed holdings												Milk-selling holdings		
	Under 25 acres			25–40 acres			Over 40 acres			Average					
	£	s.	d.	£	s.	d.	£	s.	d.	£	s.	d.	£	s.	d.
Money receipts															
Per acre ...	7	14	9	7	12	5	7	3	8	7	9	7	11	1	3
Per holding ...	173	1	10	246	13	8	330	4	11	250	15	5	427	6	10
Money expenses															
Per acre ...	4	17	3	4	13	9	4	11	9	4	13	2	6	19	5
Per holding ...	108	13	2	151	15	9	210	9	2	156	18	7	269	4	8
Balance															
Per acre ...	2	17	6	2	18	8	2	11	11	2	16	5	4	1	10
Per holding ...	64	8	8	94	17	11	119	15	9	93	16	10	158	2	2

T

of labour" and the "family unit" are practically synonymous, so that this figure is also a rough indication of the
returns per unit of labour employed as well as of the
returns per family unit. The most interesting feature
brought out from an analysis of these figures of the balance
per holding is the relatively good position shown for the
highlands. Thus, the average balance per holding in the
highlands is actually higher than it is for the mixed lowland
holdings. This is partly due to the less speculative nature
of highland husbandry, where the low bill of expense compensates for the low money income sufficiently to be
responsible for the comparatively superior result shown.
It is also partly due to the fact that the average highland
holding is larger than the average holding in the lowlands.

For the present it is proposed to defer further analysis
of these estimates of the balance per holding, since they
do not give the real net returns, although most smallholders would probably consider them as representing their
income. Before the true net return can be obtained there
are other factors to be considered which are fundamental
for its assessment. So far these have been avoided inasmuch
as they are largely theoretical conceptions which are not
represented in actual money transactions of which the
smallholder is aware. Thus, on the expense side, consideration must be given to interest on capital and to the
remuneration of family labour; and, on the income side,
account must be taken of the amount of family consumption of the produce of the holding. Each of these new
factors will now be considered in turn, and fresh tables
will be given to show the estimated gross expenses, the
estimated gross income, and the estimated net returns on
this basis.

5. THE GROSS EXPENSES

The first factor to be considered, then, is the normal interest which the smallholder should receive on the capital invested by him in the undertaking. But before this can be obtained, it is necessary to make an estimate of the amount of such capital. Throughout this study that part of the agricultural capital (usually designated as "permanent") which is represented by the value of the land and buildings has been treated as if supplied by an outside body represented by the landlord. Thus, "agricultural rent" has been charged as an item of expense to all the holdings. In this way the treatment has been considerably facilitated, although it must be admitted that the important complications attendant on the various forms of tenure have been ignored. For the present purpose, attention need only be paid to the so-called "working capital," or to that capital which the smallholder himself invests in the business. The survey did not enable an "ingoing" and an "outgoing" valuation to be made, consequently the working capital has been estimated as follows. The valuation of the stock has been made at current prices on the basis of the weighted numbers of stock on the holdings throughout the year, the method used already in the previous section. Implements and machinery have been valued at 50 per cent. of the current local prices of new articles, and in all cases a conservative estimate has been adopted. No attempt has been made to give a figure for the value of such items as tenant right, stores of provisions, etc.

The constituents of the working capital obtained in this manner are shown in detail in Table **XXXV**, which also gives their percentage distribution. The table illustrates the serious significance of the working capital in the financing of the small holding. Here, again, the regularity of the inverse movement with size and with altitude is brought out very clearly. Taking average holdings in the various

TABLE XXXV. Working capital per acre and its percentage distribution

	Highland holdings			Lowland holdings			
				Mixed holdings			Milk-selling holdings
	Under 40 acres	40–60 acres	Over 60 acres	Under 25 acres	25–40 acres	Over 40 acres	
Cattle	£ s. d. 4 7 4 *39·0 %*	£ s. d. 4 6 4 *39·1 %*	£ s. d. 2 12 4 *34·6 %*	£ s. d. 6 9 5 *46·2 %*	£ s. d. 6 12 10 *48·0 %*	£ s. d. 6 4 8 *48·1 %*	£ s. d. 8 0 10 *56·7 %*
Horses	1 0 11 *9·4 %*	0 18 6 *8·4 %*	0 12 7 *8·3 %*	1 2 4 *8·0 %*	1 7 9 *10·0 %*	1 8 9 *11·1 %*	1 2 10 *8·2 %*
Sheep	0 15 7 *7·0 %*	2 1 6 *18·8 %*	2 5 9 *30·3 %*	0 16 6 *5·9 %*	0 14 8 *5·4 %*	0 14 1 *5·4 %*	0 9 8 *3·4 %*
Pigs	0 10 3 *4·6 %*	0 7 2 *3·2 %*	0 4 7 *3·1 %*	0 16 6 *5·9 %*	0 12 8 *4·4 %*	0 12 9 *4·9 %*	0 8 8 *3·2 %*
Poultry	0 5 2 *2·3 %*	0 4 3 *1·9 %*	0 0 9 *0·5 %*	0 7 2 *2·5 %*	0 6 0 *2·3 %*	0 5 5 *2·1 %*	0 4 7 *1·4 %*
Total live stock	6 19 3 *62·3 %*	7 17 9 *71·4 %*	5 16 0 *76·8 %*	9 11 11 *68·5 %*	9 13 11 *70·1 %*	9 5 8 *71·6 %*	10 6 7 *72·9 %*
Implements and machinery	4 4 5 *37·7 %*	3 3 2 *28·6 %*	1 15 0 *23·2 %*	4 8 4 *31·5 %*	4 2 9 *29·9 %*	3 13 6 *28·4 %*	3 16 6 *27·1 %*
Total	11 3 8 *100·0 %*	11 0 11 *100·0 %*	7 11 0 *100·0 %*	14 0 3 *100·0 %*	13 16 8 *100·0 %*	12 19 2 *100·0 %*	14 3 1 *100·0 %*

groups, we find that a 35 acre holding in the highlands requires a total working capital of approximately £341, or £11 per acre, the corresponding figures for a mixed lowland holding of 22 acres is £308, or £14 per acre, while an average holding of 38·5 acres in the milk-selling group requires an approximate total working capital of £545, or just over £14 an acre.

The relatively higher degree of working capital on the smaller holdings is due to the comparatively higher cost of equipping them with the necessary implements and machinery. While this is true of both highland and lowland holdings, the table illustrates it best for the highland groups where implements and machinery account for 37·7 per cent. of the total working capital of holdings under 40 acres in extent, but only for 23·2 per cent. of the total working capital of holdings over 60 acres in extent. The allocation of the capital per acre between the various types of machinery was as follows:

	Group A 1			Group A 2			Group A 3			Group B 1			Group B 2			Group B 3			Group C		
	£	s.	d.	£	s.	d.	£	s.	d.	£	s.	d.	£	s.	d.	£	s.	d.	£	s.	d.
Vehicles	1	7	6	0	16	7	0	8	2	1	5	3	1	0	10	0	17	5	0	18	9
Cultivating implements	0	8	9	0	8	1	0	4	3	0	7	1	0	9	5	0	6	10	0	6	10
Harvesting machines	0	16	2	0	12	6	0	6	9	0	12	9	0	14	3	0	16	6	0	19	2
Barn machinery	0	11	5	0	8	4	0	3	10	0	9	9	0	9	10	0	7	6	0	6	0
Dairy utensils	0	7	6	0	4	7	0	2	8	0	10	10	0	8	1	0	5	10	0	8	9
Power	0	1	9	0	4	6	0	3	6	0	6	9	0	7	6	0	10	0	0	5	4
Tools, etc.	0	4	2	0	3	0	0	1	8	0	6	9	0	4	8	0	3	2	0	4	11
Harness	0	7	2	0	5	7	0	4	2	0	9	2	0	8	2	0	6	3	0	6	9
Total	4	4	5	3	3	2	1	15	0	4	8	4	4	2	9	3	13	6	3	16	6

The highest item in all groups (except C) is the cost of vehicles. The highland smallholder has to pay more for his cultivating implements to meet his relatively greater arable area. Harvesting machinery accounts for a relatively higher amount of capital on the smaller holdings, while there is less variation from group to group in the cost of barn or food preparing machinery. The cost of dairy utensils falls with the rise in acreage, being relatively higher for the lowland holdings. This is also the case for the cost of harness as well as of small implements and tools. The figure given for capital invested in power has to be taken carefully since it is unduly affected for the various groups by individual holdings equipped either with water wheels or with oil engine plants.

The proportion of the working capital invested in live stock being the complement of that invested in implements and machinery, it follows that live stock represents a relatively greater amount of the working capital of the lowland holdings, and this is shown to be so in Table **XXXV**. The table further shows that the actual amount per acre invested in live stock is considerably higher in the lowlands, and this is true of each branch with the exception of sheep, the capital in which is naturally higher on the highland holdings.

The amount of capital invested in cattle is the predominant item in all groups, and in the case of milk-selling holdings it accounts for over 56 per cent. of the total working capital. The value of horses accounts for over 8 per cent. of the working capital in all groups. This is a serious item on the small holding, since (as in the case of capital invested in implements and machinery) the return from it is much less apparent. For both highland and lowland holdings it moves inversely to the acreage. While sheep account for only a little over 5 per cent. of the working capital of the lowland holdings, and for only 7 per cent. in the first highland group, they are of much greater significance on the larger highland holdings, making up 30·3 per cent. of the total agricultural capital of the holdings over 60 acres in extent. What makes both pigs and poultry peculiarly suitable for small scale farming is

that the turnover obtained from them is great in comparison to the capital invested. The table shows this
capital to be relatively small for all groups, and it also
shows it to be comparatively higher, first, on the smaller
than on the larger holdings, and second, on the lowland
than on the highland farms.

After this necessary digression on the capitalisation of
small holdings, it is possible to proceed with a discussion
of the real gross expenses per acre shown in the next table.

TABLE XXXVI.   Gross expenses per acre

	Group A 1			Group A 2			Group A 3			Group B 1			Group B 2			Group B 3			Group C		
	£	s.	d.	£	s.	d.	£	s.	d.	£	s.	d.	£	s.	d.	£	s.	d.	£	s.	d.
Money expenses	2	13	1	2	14	10	1	11	6	4	17	3	4	13	9	4	11	9	6	19	5
Normal interest	0	11	2	0	11	1	0	7	6	0	14	0	0	13	10	0	12	11	0	14	2
Family wages	3	16	3	3	1	9	1	19	10	5	5	0	3	18	4	3	2	6	3	14	6
Gross expenses	7	0	6	6	7	8	3	18	10	10	16	3	9	5	11	8	7	2	11	8	1

The figure given for the normal interest on capital has
been obtained by charging a rate of 5 per cent. on the
working capital shown in Table XXXV. It follows, therefore, that the movements from group to group in the
amounts of this interest will correspond to those already
traced for the working capital itself.

The amounts given as family wages require very careful
interpretation, and have only been introduced to complete
the conception of a theoretical net profit. There was no
statutory rate of minimum wages in operation in respect
of agricultural labourers in Carmarthenshire during the
year 1923. From the available information, however, it

appears that the wages of general labourers at this period varied between 28 shillings and 32 shillings per week[1]. This is closely corroborated by the limited number of cases in the present survey in which hired labour was employed. In order, therefore, to obtain as conservative an estimate as possible, the lower limit of 28 shillings per week has been used as the basis for assessing the remuneration of the family for its labour on the holding[2]. The depressing effect on the income of rewarding family labour in this manner is seen to be considerable, being very great on the smaller holdings where the labour bill per acre becomes very formidable. It is, however, dangerous to infer too much from this, since there are many points of difference between family and hired labour which must be remembered. The most important, probably, is the fact that in the case of these small holdings the amount of labour employed is not determined so much by the amount of work to be done as by the amount of labour available. Thus, in the case of the small family farm the available labour is determined by the size of the family, and all this will be utilised even if not fully. A simple illustration will help to emphasise this point. Two holdings, exactly similar in all respects, will have different labour bills, if, on the one, the family consists of man and wife only, while, on the other, three children also assist with the work of the holding. Although, possibly, the man and wife work harder on the first holding to obtain the same result, the important consideration is the fact that in the absence of the three children on the second holding, no hired labour would have been engaged to complete the labour equipment of

---

[1] This information has been kindly supplied by the Ministry of Agriculture and Fisheries.

[2] Female labour is assessed at 60 per cent. and child labour at 20 per cent. of the value of male labour.

the holding. While this is an indication of the danger of assessing family labour at current rates of wages, it also serves to show the necessity for holdings large enough to give full time employment to the basis of the family unit, that is to a man and wife.

6. THE GROSS INCOME

To obtain the correct value of the gross income it is necessary to supplement the money income already shown in Table XXVII by the value of the produce of the holding consumed by the family. This necessary adjustment is

TABLE XXXVII. Gross income per acre

	Group A 1			Group A 2			Group A 3			Group B 1			Group B 2			Group B 3			Group C		
	£	s.	d.	£	s.	d.	£	s.	d.	£	s.	d.	£	s.	d.	£	s.	d.	£	s.	d.
Money income or gross sales	5	7	7	5	4	1	3	8	1	7	14	9	7	12	5	7	3	8	11	1	3
Value of produce consumed by family	1	1	2	0	15	10	0	9	10	1	9	10	1	0	5	0	15	10	0	18	11
Do. as per cent. of gross income	16·5 %			13·2 %			12·8 %			16·2 %			11·8 %			9·9 %			7·9 %		
Gross income	6	8	9	5	19	11	3	17	11	9	4	7	8	12	10	7	19	6	12	0	2

given in detail in the above table, which also gives the percentage which the value of this home-consumed produce forms of the gross incomes of the various groups.

Exact information of the amount of the family consumption of the various farm produce was given for only seven holdings. There is every reason to believe, however, that these are sufficiently representative to justify their use as a basis for assessing the amounts in the other cases. In practically every case the holding supplies the family with its total consumption of milk, butter, eggs, poultry, bacon, potatoes, and garden produce[1]. The table shows how the value of this per acre falls with the rise in the size of both highland and lowland holdings. This is only to be expected since it depends almost entirely on the number of people maintained per acre, a factor which manifests a similar movement. The table also shows the percentage which the value of the amounts consumed by the family form of the value of the total production of the holding. Here again there is a fall with the rise in acreage, and in no case is it over 16·5 per cent. It is clear, therefore, that the production of foodstuffs for sale is the primary object of these small holdings; although, at the same time, they are practically self-contained as far as the foodstuffs enumerated above are concerned. Moreover, the value of such foodstuffs consumed by the household must necessarily be an important consideration in estimating the standard of living of the smallholder and his family[2].

7. NET RETURNS PER ACRE

When the value of the gross expenses per acre shown in Table XXXVI is deducted from the value of the gross income per acre shown in Table XXXVII, the result gives the value of the net returns per acre which is shown in the next table.

[1] Analysis of the available data gives an average of £35 per annum as the value of produce consumed off the holding by a family of man and wife and one school child.

[2] Some other items, such as the value of the house, fuel, etc., which also affect the standard of living, have had to be omitted because of insufficient data concerning them.

TABLE XXXVIII. Net returns per acre

	Highland holdings			
	Under 40 acres	40–60 acres	Over 60 acres	Average
	£ s. d.	£ s. d.	£ s. d.	£ s. d.
Gross income	6 8 9	5 19 11	3 17 11	5 3 1
Gross expenses	7 0 6	6 7 8	3 18 10	5 10 0
Net returns	(−)0 11 9	(−)0 7 9	(−)0 0 11	(−)0 6 11

	Lowland holdings				
	Mixed holdings				Milk-selling holdings
	Under 25 acres	25–40 acres	Over 40 acres	Average	
	£ s. d.	£ s. d.	£ s. d.	£ s. d.	£ s. d.
Gross income	9 4 7	8 12 10	7 19 6	8 9 10	12 0 2
Gross expenses	10 16 3	9 5 11	8 7 2	9 4 0	11 8 1
Net returns	(−)1 11 8	(−)0 13 1	(−)0 7 8	(−)0 14 2	0 12 1

The estimates of the net returns per acre given in this table present a marked contrast to the figures of the balance of money expenses and money receipts given earlier in Table XXXIV. Thus it will be seen that the milk-selling group alone possesses a clear profit per acre after all other expenses, including interest on capital and family wages, have been allowed for. In all the other groups there is an adverse balance per acre, and this is most unfavourable for the smallest holdings, the lowland holdings under 25 acres showing an actual deficit of £1. 11s. 8d. per acre. However, these unfavourable results are almost entirely due to the disturbing effect of the family wages on the bill of expense, and, in view of what has already been said regarding the limits of this factor, it is not very safe to draw many deductions from this table. The net balance per acre, which the table professes to show, may be taken as a gauge of the results when land is the factor of production under discussion.

In this place it is convenient to attempt to arrive at a standard of efficiency in the use of capital, a second factor of production to be considered. This may be fairly easily done by deducting all expenses (with the exception of normal interest on capital) from the total income. The resulting figure represents the amount which the smallholder receives as gross interest on the capital invested by him in the undertaking. The necessary standard is then obtained by expressing this amount as a percentage of the working capital itself. The result of calculating this is as follows for the various groups:

	Gross interest as percentage of working capital
Group A 1 ...	(−) 0·26
„ A 2 ...	1·51
„ A 3 ...	4·36
Group B 1 ...	(−) 6·30
„ B 2 ...	0·27
„ B 3 ...	1·89
Group C ...	9·33

In order to appreciate the full significance of these figures it is necessary to bear in mind two important considerations. The first, here again, is the influence of the estimated family wage in arriving at the results, since this undoubtedly accounts for the adverse ratio obtaining on the smallest holdings in both highlands and lowlands. The second factor which tells unfavourably on the smaller farms is their comparatively higher capitalisation, although a too conservative estimate of the working capital at the start may possibly be now responsible for a generous error in the calculation of the rate of interest obtained on that capital. The figures indicate that there is a better return per unit of capital as the holdings increase in size in both the highland and the lowland groups, while the milk-selling holdings, with a rate of interest of 9·33 per cent., are here again shown to occupy both actually and comparatively a very favourable position.

8. NET RETURNS PER HOLDING

The more practical discussion of the net returns per holding, or per family unit, still remains, and the details necessary for this are set out in Table XXXIX.

TABLE XXXIX. Net returns per holding

	Highland holdings			
	Under 40 acres	40–60 acres	Over 60 acres	Average
	£ s. d.	£ s. d.	£ s. d.	£ s. d.
Gross income	223 13 7	291 7 11	346 14 7	280 19 6
Gross expenses	244 9 5	310 4 7	350 16 2	300 6 0
Net returns	(−) 20 15 10	(−) 18 16 8	(−) 4 1 7	(−) 19 6 6

	Lowland holdings				
	Mixed holdings				Milk-selling holdings
	Under 25 acres	25–40 acres	Over 40 acres	Average	
	£ s. d.	£ s. d.	£ s. d.	£ s. d.	£ s. d.
Gross income	205 16 2	279 19 9	366 2 11	284 17 9	463 12 0
Gross expenses	241 2 5	301 3 8	383 12 11	309 2 5	440 4 0
Net returns	(−) 35 6 3	(−) 21 3 11	(−) 17 10 0	(−) 24 4 8	23 8 0

Inasmuch as the figures in this table have been obtained in exactly the same way as the estimates of the net returns per acre already given, it follows that they exhibit the same general tendency, and are also subject to the same limitations of interpretation. Thus it will be seen that the milk-selling group is the only one with a clear profit per holding after all expenses including normal interest have been met, while the adverse balance is heaviest for the smaller holdings in both highlands and lowlands.

The real importance of the table, however, rests with the introduction it affords for a study of the remuneration of labour, the factor of production which still remains to be discussed. For this purpose it is convenient to apply to labour an analogous treatment to that already applied in the case of capital. Thus, if instead of considering the remuneration of family labour as an expense it is added to the net returns shown in Table XXXIX, the figure resulting may be regarded as the "family wages." The result of computing this for the various groups is as follows:

	Family wages			Wages per unit of labour		
	£	s.	d.	£	s.	d.
Group A 1 ...	111	17	8	50	0	9
„ A 2 ...	123	3	4	51	2	9
„ A 3 ...	173	3	7	60	4	9
Average A 1–A 3	132	13	8	53	5	9
Group B 1 ...	81	15	3	42	2	11
„ B 2 ...	106	3	1	51	15	8
„ B 3 ...	125	19	7	58	6	6
Average B 1–B 3	105	7	7	51	8	1
Group C ...	167	3	8	66	16	7

Such a conception of family wages has much to recommend itself as a criterion of the value of the relative standard of living of the various groups, particularly since there is a marked similarity in the size of the family throughout. These figures show the highland small holding in a very favourable light, since the average weekly family earnings on the highland small holdings are 51*s.*, while the corresponding average for the mixed lowland holdings is 40*s.* 6*d.* The family wage is highest for the milk-selling group, and lowest for the small lowland holdings of under 25 acres. These figures are useful when conclusions have to be drawn as to the relative economic status of the smallholder and the agricultural labourer.

In discussing the reward of the unit of labour employed it is, perhaps, more correct to limit considerations to the figures given in the second column of the table above. These figures show the reward obtained per unit employed, both hired and family labour having been converted into a common unit, viz. "men equivalents."[1] The general movement from group to group is seen to be closely similar to the movement in the amount of the family wages, while the family wage itself is slightly over twice as large as the reward per unit of labour for each of the groups. This result follows necessarily from the similarity throughout in the size of the family which carries an average complement of 2·1 units of labour. It is necessary, before closing this discussion on the reward of labour, to note that no separate treatment has been given to the remuneration of management. The difficulty of differentiating satisfactorily between the wages of management and the wages of manual labour is very great even in large scale agricultural production. In the case of the small holding it becomes practically impossible. Moreover, at the outset of this study, the absence of any differentiation of function as between manager and manual worker was considered to be one of the most satisfactory distinguishing characteristics of the small holding.

[1] The scale of conversion into "men equivalents" is the same as that used on page 54.

D. SUMMARY

Without attempting to generalise, the results of this study supply useful information on several important aspects of the work and life of the smallholders of an extensive area, and it is, therefore, convenient to summarise in this place the more important of these.

The first part contains much information regarding the relation between the size of holdings and their crops, live stock, employment, and general equipment. Thus the amount of arable land has been shown to be small and comparatively unimportant throughout. A tendency for it to increase with the size of the holding has, however, been shown. Again, a characteristic of the stocking of the holding, emphasised by the study, is the superiority of the "stock carrying" capacity of the smaller over the larger holdings. The importance of cattle, pigs, and poultry on the small farm has also been brought out, as well as the serious significance of the horse problem. Lastly, figures have been given to illustrate the fact that the smaller holdings provide much more employment to the acre than do the large farms.

It is also very instructive to compare the relative cropping and stocking of the highland and lowland holdings in relation to their rental. Thus, in the highlands with an average rent of 14s. 9d. per acre the average stock carried is equivalent to 35·5 "animal units" to the acre, while the corresponding figures for the lowlands are £1. 10s. 5d. and 48·5 "animal units" respectively. Looked at in this way the strange result is obtained that the highland holdings carry a larger head of stock to the unit of rent. There are many factors to be considered in explaining this result. It is due partly to the greater percentage of arable land in the highlands, and this again is necessitated partly by the poorer quality of the soil and the consequent need for the produce of the crops to maintain the live stock. On the other hand, it is probable that a superior class of stock is kept in the lowlands, with a corresponding superiority in the productive efficiency of the stock units. Lastly, due weight must also be given to the arbitrary nature of the scale used in converting the various classes of stock into "animal units." It is certain, however, that this apparent superior stock-carrying capacity of the highland small holdings has much to do with their relatively good position as shown by the analysis of the financial accounts.

As regards the second part of the study, the first thing to be noted is the detailed analysis given of the nature and money values of the various items of sales and of expenses. The predominant source of income on all the holdings is the cattle economy, and particularly dairying. In view of the good position occupied by the milk-selling group, it seems that a development of this type is desirable. Not only is the income of the smallholder higher on the milk-selling holdings, but the work of the housewife is considerably lessened by the absence of the domestic system of butter-making. Any increase in the number of holdings selling milk, however, must necessitate the contemporaneous development of a co-operative system for the collection and for the utilisation of this product. Next to cattle, pigs and poultry are the important factors in producing the smallholder's income, and, generally speaking, more specialised attention to these branches would greatly improve his financial position. Here it is possible to suggest as a general criticism of the present organisation of most of the small holdings, that it is too often merely a copy on a small scale of large farming practice, whereas

the real interest of the smallholder lies in a certain degree
of specialisation in those branches of husbandry which are
best adapted to small scale organisation.

The most serious problem of the smallholder is that of
his relatively high expenses, resulting from the high
interest demanded by his comparatively large capital, his
heavy purchases of feeding stuffs, and his high labour bill
when his own labour and that of his family are adequately
recompensed. All these have been amply illustrated during
the course of the study. The heavy bill for feeding stuffs
points to the smallholder's need for an adequate system
of co-operative purchase of his chief requisites, while the
development of a suitable system of credit organisation
would go far to meet the other difficulties mentioned.

The influence of the size of the holding both on the sales
per acre and on the expenses per acre have been repeatedly
observed, both sales and expenses manifesting an inverse
ratio to the size of the holding. Similarly, the relations
of these two factors to the altitude have also been emphasised, both the sales per acre and the expenses per
acre being considerably higher for the lowlands than for
the highlands.

The most important feature of the whole study is, perhaps, the attempt made to arrive at an approximation
of the net returns of the various groups. The need for
approaching this on the basis of the various factors of
production has been shown, so also has the difficulty of
obtaining a satisfactory standard for comparison. The
arbitrary nature of the estimation of such important influences as interest on capital, value of home-consumed
produce, and remuneration of family labour, makes it
impossible to arrive at an exact figure of the net returns
of the small holdings. Nevertheless, certain general
tendencies are to be distinguished in the results obtained.

Thus, only the milk-selling holdings show a surplus per acre after all expenses, including family wages, have been met. In the case of the other holdings, the actual deficit per acre is less in the highlands than in the lowlands, while there is a tendency throughout for it to increase as the holdings become smaller in size. This comparatively favourable position of the highland holdings has been shown to be due mostly to their less speculative nature, their lower expenses per acre compensating for their lower production. Again, the comparatively unfavourable position of the smaller holdings in both highlands and lowlands is almost entirely due to the disproportionate size of their labour bills. So much depends on the influence of this labour bill that it is advisable to confine the final examination to the reward of labour itself. Both the family earnings and the earnings per unit of labour employed have been shown to increase with the size of the holding; the highland holdings have been shown to occupy a very favourable position, although the best results obtain for the milk-selling holdings. It is tempting to give a comparison of these earnings with the earnings of the agricultural labourer, and, so far as the results go, there does not seem to be very much difference between the two. Although the reward per unit of labour is higher in the case of the agricultural labourer, on the other hand the total family earnings of the smallholder are considerably higher. This, however, is very inadequate as a comparison of the relative standard of living of smallholders and farm labourers, since so many other factors, which cannot be assessed in money values, enter into the conception of the standard of living. Nevertheless, it is clear that for every type of small holding there is a lower limit of size, and as this is approached it becomes less certain that the smallholder will receive an adequate reward for his labour.

The smaller holdings included in the survey are probably not far removed from this lower limit. A comparison of the highland and lowland groups shows how the quality of the land is one of the factors determining this, it being clear that the limit is considerably higher in the case of the highland groups. The chief determinant of this limit, however, is probably the type of farming pursued. Thus it is clear from this survey that small holdings of the type most generally found in Carmarthenshire, i.e., those which adopt farming systems prevalent on and suitable for the medium and large scale farms, soon reach their lower limit for this very reason. This is borne out by the fact that the larger of the small holdings considered here seem to provide their occupiers with a higher remuneration than that which is obtained by the occupiers of the smaller holdings, whereas in all cases the system of farming is that practised on larger farms. It is not safe, however, to argue from this that the smaller holdings are uneconomic units, since such an argument holds good only in so far as the smallholder persists in making his holding a small scale plan of the large farm. When, and only when, the smallholder concentrates on those special branches of farming that he can conduct, not merely as well as but even better than the large scale farmer, can he hope to make his holding an economic unit of production. Meanwhile, there can be but little doubt that it would repay him to tighten up his general system of management, since at present this can hardly be described as intensive. It seems, however, that the great problem in the development of the native type of small holding in Carmarthenshire, as well as in Wales generally, is the need for evolving some system or systems of cultivation and live stock production specially suitable for small scale organisation.

APPENDIX A

BIBLIOGRAPHY

SECTION I

ADAMS, W. G. S. *Some Considerations Relating to the Position of the Small Holding in the United Kingdom.* Journal of the Royal Statistical Society, vol. LXX, part III, 1907.

ASHBY, ARTHUR W. *Allotments and Small Holdings in Oxfordshire.* Clarendon Press, Oxford, 1917.

—— *Small Holdings and Corn Prices.* Economic Journal, vol. XXVII, 1917.

BENNETT, E. N. *Problems of Village Life.* Williams & Norgate, London. N.D. Chapter VIII on "Small Holdings."

DUNCAN, JOSEPH F. *Agriculture and the Community.* International Bookshops, Ltd., Glasgow, 1921. Chapter II on "Some Present Day Policies—Small Holdings."

HALL, A. D. *Agriculture after the War.* John Murray, London, 1920. Chapter IV on "Possible Developments.—Industrialised Farms, Small Holding Colonies."

HARBEN, HENRY D. *The Rural Problem.* Constable & Co., Ltd., London, 1913. Chapter VI on "Small Holdings."

LEVY, HERMANN. *Large and Small Holdings*—A Study of English Agricultural Economics. English Translation by Ruth Kenyon. Cambridge University Press, 1911.

ORWIN, C. S. *The Small Holdings Craze.* Edinburgh Review, April 1916.

PIGOU, A. C. *Essays in Applied Economics.* P. S. King & Son, London, 1923. Chapter IX on "Small Holdings."

PRYSE-HOWELL, J. *Large and Small Holdings.* Welsh Outlook, January 1922.

TURNER, CHRISTOPHER. *Our Food Supply*. Country Life Library, London, 1916. Chapter v on "Small Holdings."
—— *The Land and its Problems*. Methuen & Co., Ltd., London, 1921. Chapter vi on "Small and Large Holdings."

VENN, J. A. *Foundations of Agricultural Economics*. Cambridge University Press, 1923. Chapters iii and iv on "The Size of Holdings."

Final Report of *The Agricultural Tribunal of Investigation*. Cmd. 2145, 1924.

Interim Report on *The Economics of Small Farms and Small Holdings in Scotland*. Edinburgh, 1919.

The Land.—*The Report of the Land Enquiry Committee*. Vol. i. Rural. Hodder and Stoughton, London, 1913. Chapter iii on "Small Holdings."

SECTION II

DAVIES, WALTER. *General View of the Domestic Economy of South Wales*. Drawn up for the consideration of the Board of Agriculture and Internal Improvement. London, 1815.

HASSAL, CHARLES. *General View of the Agriculture of the County of Carmarthen*. W. Smith, London, 1794.

JONES, C. BRYNER. *Small Holdings in Wales*. Welsh Housing and Development Year Book. 1924.

MORGAN, DAVID. *The Story of Carmarthenshire*. Educational Publishing Co., Cardiff, 1909.

PRYSE-HOWELL, J. *An Economic Survey of a Rural Parish* Oxford University Press, 1923.

SPURRELL, W. *General History of the County of Carmarthen*. Spurrell, Carmarthen, 1879.

THOMAS, D. LLEUFER. *Welsh Land Commission—A Digest of its Report*. Whittaker & Co., London, 1896.

Agricultural Statistics. 1885 to 1924.

Annual Report of *Proceedings under the Small Holdings and Allotments Act* 1908. Part i. Cd. 7851, 1915.

Report on *Land Settlement in England and Wales* 1919 *to* 1924. (1926.)

Report of *Proceedings under the Small Holdings Colonies Acts* (1916 *and* 1918) *and the Sailors and Soldiers (Gift of Land Settlement) Act* 1916.

Report of the *Royal Commission on Land in Wales and Monmouthshire.* C. 8221, 1896.

Report on *Wages and Conditions of Employment in Agriculture.* Vols. I and II, Cmd. 24, Cmd. 25, 1919.

1921 *Census Reports.*

APPENDIX B

LIST OF TABLES

APPENDIX C

SUMMARIES OF COMPARABLE STUDIES ABROAD

1. Sources and Classification

In this appendix it is proposed to give summaries of the results of investigations, of a nature similar to the one just described in detail, which have been conducted in the four European countries of Denmark, Norway, Sweden, and Switzerland. In each of these countries research has for years been directed towards the elucidation of the problem of the economic size of the farm holding, and the data that have been collected supply, therefore, valuable information on the relative efficiency of large and small agricultural enterprises.

A comparison of the results from these countries with the result of the Carmarthenshire survey is made still more interesting since in each of these countries the small family farm is the prevailing type of agricultural organisation. The percentage division of holdings according to the official statistics is given for each country in the following table, which helps to demonstrate the predominance of the small holding in their farming economy.

Thus, it shows that if 75 acres be taken as the dividing line between large and small holdings, then the percentage of large farms is practically negligible for all the continental countries except Denmark, and even in that country only 13·4 per cent. of the holdings are in the larger size-group. When measured by the usual standard of acreage, therefore, the farms in these countries are divided into remarkably small lots, and they are specially suitable for the study of the economics of the small unit of production in agriculture[1].

[1] To appreciate the position properly it must be remembered, however, that husbandry in these countries, particularly in Scandinavia, affords excellent opportunities for accessory sources of income. For example, in the case of Norway it has been established that if the holdings are divided into farms and small holdings, then 52·2 per cent. of the farms have some extra source of profit, while only 10·9 per cent. of the small holdings are

TABLE A. Percentage distribution of agricultural holdings in Denmark, Norway, Sweden, Switzerland, and Wales

	Denmark*	Norway†	Sweden‡	Switzer-land§	Wales‖
Acres Under 25	% 53·0	% 93·7	% 76·9	% 82·8	Under 100 acres 87·2 %
25–75	33·6	5·7	18·6	14·2	Over 100 acres 12·8 %
Over 75	13·4	0·6	4·5	3·0	—
Total	100·0	100·0	100·0	100·0	100·0

* *Danmarks Statistisk Aarbog*, 1923, p. 42.
† *Norges Offisielle Statistikk*. VII, 12. (*Jordbrukstellingen i Norge*, 1 Jan. 1918, p. 21.)
‡ *Arealinventeringen och Husdjursrakningen den 1. Juni 1919, av Kungl. Statistiska Centralbyran*, II, p. 4.
§ *Ergebnisse der eidg. Betriebszahlung vom 9. Aug. 1905. Band 2. (Schweizerische Statistik, 168. Lieferung.)*
‖ *Agricultural Statistics*, 1923, Part I.

The material which forms the basis of this section has been extracted from the annual reports for the year 1922–23 of institutes of research in agricultural economics in these four countries[1]. At the outset it is very important to realise the limitation which must be observed in drawing conclusions from these various reports. In so far as they represent the position of large and small farms in their respective countries

without such extra source, and the holding itself is of secondary importance in the case of 65·5 per cent. of the remainder. See *De Faste Eiendommer i arene 1916–1920, Norges Offisielle Statistikk.* VII, 89, p. 50.

[1] The full references are as follows:

(1) *Undersøgelser over Landbrugets Driftsforhold*, VII in *Aaret* 1922–23, prepared by Det Landokonomiske Driftsbureau, Copenhagen (1924).
(2) *Regnskapresultater fra Norske Gardsbruk*, 15, 1922–23, prepared by Det Kgl. Selskap for Norges Vel. Fredrikshald (1924).
(3) *Räkenskapresultat från Svenska Jordbruk*, IX, 1922–23, prepared by Kungl. Lantdruksstyrelsen, Malmö (1925).
(4) *Untersuchungen betreffend die Rentabilität der schweizerischen Landwirtschaft*, 1922–23, des schweizerischen Bauernsekretariates, Berne (1924).

These are hereinafter referred to as Danish Report, Norwegian Report, Swedish Report, and Swiss Report, respectively.

they are of course unassailable. But the notorious difficulty of comparing the production, or the standard of living of producers, in any two countries makes it almost unnecessary to emphasise the extreme care with which they must be used in attempting any such comparisons. A primary cause of this difficulty is due to the many differences in the technique of the methods of compiling the statistical data employed in the various countries. An example of this is afforded at the start in the variety of acreage classifications used. It has been possible, fortunately for the present purpose, to select three groups of holdings in each country which are approximately comparable on an acreage basis. The selection is shown in the following table, which gives for each country the classification

	Denmark*		Norway†		Sweden‡		Switzerland§		Carmarthen-shire	
	Size group (acres)	No. in group	Size group (acres)	No. in group	Size group (acres)	No. in group	Size group (acres)	No. in group	Size group (acres)	No. in group
Group A	Under 25	45	Under 25	6	Under 25	26	12·5–25	158	Under 25	13
Group B	25–50	88	25–50	17	25–62·5	16	25–37·5	91	25–40	24
Group C	50–75	121	50–75	17	62·5–125	4	37·5–75	90	Over 40	14
Total	—	254	—	40	—	46	—	339	—	51

* Danish Report, Table 13, p. 26.
† Norwegian Report, Hovedtabell III, p. 91.
‡ Swedish Report, Table 4, p. 10.
§ Swiss Report, Table on p. 30. The conversion scale used is 1 hectare = 2·47 acres.

together with the number of holdings in each group covered by the study.

The acreage grouping is identical for Denmark and Norway, but there are slight deviations for both Sweden and Switzerland. It should also be stated that, whereas the Danish and Swiss figures are for holdings scattered all over those countries, the Norwegian figures apply only to the eastern part of Norway, and the Swedish figures to central Sweden only. This is due to the fact that for the two latter countries the reports deal with separate districts, and the averages for the whole country are not given on an acreage basis. This is presumably due to the great difficulty, even within one country, of correlating results which are so very varied in their nature. The mixed lowland holdings in the Carmarthenshire survey have been added to complete the table, and, where necessary in the following discussion, attention will be drawn to any points of difference which may exist for the highland holdings, or for the milk-selling group.

2. GROSS PRODUCTION

The first use which can be made of this mass of information is to show the influence of the size of the holding on its total production. The next comprehensive table has been prepared to illustrate this for each country, and it shows the money value of the gross output per acre together with its percentage distribution between the various branches of the farm[1].

The table shows that the value of the gross output per acre falls from the first to the third group in each country. For the three Scandinavian countries the difference between the gross production of the first and second group is much greater than the corresponding difference between the second and the third group. For Switzerland, on the other hand, the reverse is the case, and this is probably due to the lower acreage limit of the second group here. However, as far as the total value of the gross production is concerned, the evidence of the table seems to be conclusive, there being very little doubt of the superiority of the smaller holdings.

[1] The money values in Table B, as well as in other tables in this section, have been obtained by converting the different currencies into terms of the £ sterling at the following rates:

Denmark	...	...	21·29 kroner to the £1
Norway	...	...	25·23 kroner to the £1
Sweden	...	...	16·96 kroner to the £1
Switzerland	...	...	22·98 francs to the £1

These represent, approximately, the average rates of the exchanges for 1922.

TABLE B. Gross output per acre, and percentage distribution of gross output.

	Denmark*			Norway†			Sweden†		
	A	B	C	A	B	C	A	B	C
	£ s. d.	£ s. d.	£ s. d.	£ s. d.	£ s. d.	£ s. d.	£ s. d.	£ s. d.	£ s. d.
Crops ...	1 11 7 *6·7 %*	1 4 4 *6·8 %*	1 13 5 *10·1 %*	3 7 1 *18·4 %*	3 2 11 *22·4 %*	2 14 7 *22·3 %*	1 2 5 *9·1 %*	1 4 4 *14·4 %*	1 18 8 *19·8 %*
Dairy produce ...	8 9 7 *35·9 %*	7 0 4 *39·0 %*	6 3 7 *37·1 %*	9 0 1 *49·5 %*	6 14 3 *47·7 %*	5 3 1 *42·3 %*	4 11 8 *37·4 %*	3 10 2 *41·4 %*	4 14 0 *48·1 %*
Other from cattle ...	1 18 9 *8·1 %*	1 15 4 *10·0 %*	1 11 11 *9·6 %*	0 18 8 *5·2 %*	1 9 6 *10·6 %*	1 3 5 *9·5 %*	1 8 7 *11·7 %*	0 16 3 *9·6 %*	0 19 7 *10·0 %*
Total cattle ...	10 8 4 *44·0 %*	8 15 8 *49·0 %*	7 15 6 *46·7 %*	9 18 9 *54·7 %*	8 3 9 *58·3 %*	6 6 6 *51·8 %*	6 0 3 *49·1 %*	4 6 5 *51·0 %*	5 13 7 *58·1 %*
Horses ...	0 1 6 *0·3 %*	0 4 7 *1·3 %*	0 3 10 *1·1 %*	1 0 7 *5·6 %*	0 8 8 *3·1 %*	0 14 2 *6·0 %*	—	—	—
Sheep ...	—	—	—	0 6 5 *1·8 %*	0 1 3 *0·4 %*	0 3 10 *1·5 %*	—	—	—
Pigs ...	7 14 4 *32·7 %*	5 16 0 *32·4 %*	5 11 9 *33·6 %*	0 17 0 *4·7 %*	0 14 9 *5·3 %*	1 0 10 *8·5 %*	2 8 3 *19·6 %*	1 6 9 *15·8 %*	0 11 11 *6·1 %*
Poultry ...	2 9 10 *10·6 %*	1 1 8 *6·1 %*	0 14 10 *4·5 %*	0 14 5 *4·0 %*	0 7 8 *2·8 %*	0 3 10 *1·6 %*	—	—	—
Other stock ...	0 0 5 *0·1 %*	0 0 9 *0·2 %*	0 1 2 *0·3 %*	0 0 4 *0·1 %*	0 0 4 *0·1 %*	0 0 8 *0·3 %*	1 16 9 *15·0 %*	1 1 11 *12·9 %*	0 14 4 *7·3 %*
Live stock and live stock products ...	20 14 5 *87·7 %*	15 18 8 *89·0 %*	14 7 1 *86·2 %*	12 17 6 *70·9 %*	9 16 5 *70·0 %*	8 9 10 *69·7 %*	10 5 3 *83·7 %*	6 15 1 *79·7 %*	6 19 10 *71·5 %*
Other sources ...	1 7 0 *5·6 %*	0 15 3 *4·2 %*	0 12 7 *3·7 %*	1 18 10 *10·7 %*	1 1 6 *7·6 %*	0 19 7 *8·0 %*	0 17 8 *7·2 %*	0 10 1 *5·9 %*	0 17 2 *8·7 %*
Total ...	23 13 0	17 18 3	16 13 1	18 3 5	14 0 10	12 4 0	12 5 4	8 9 6	9 15 8

	Switzerland§			Carmarthenshire		
	A	B	C	A	B	C
	£ s. d.	£ s. d.	£ s. d.	£ s. d.	£ s. d.	£ s. d.
Crops	2 3 4 10·5%	1 19 1 9·8%	2 1 11 11·9%	0 0 1 0·0%	0 1 9 1·1%	0 0 1 0·1%
Dairy produce ...	6 10 8 31·6%	6 15 2 33·8%	6 9 3 36·8%	2 1 4 26·7%	2 3 2 28·3%	2 4 10 31·2%
Other from cattle ...	3 9 0 16·6%	3 1 11 15·5%	2 12 9 15·1%	1 19 2 25·3%	2 0 3 26·4%	2 3 6 30·1%
Total cattle ...	9 19 8 48·2%	9 17 1 49·3%	9 2 0 51·9%	4 0 6 52·0%	4 3 5 54·7%	4 8 4 61·3%
Horses	0 6 8 1·6%	0 11 3 2·7%	0 13 5 3·8%	0 0 6 0·3%	0 4 10 3·2%	0 2 8 1·9%
Sheep	0 1 1 0·3%	0 0 5 0·1%	0 0 9 0·2%	0 10 10 7·0%	0 10 2 6·7%	0 12 1 8·4%
Pigs	1 13 5 8·1%	1 19 5 9·8%	1 6 5 7·5%	1 12 9 21·2%	1 8 5 18·6%	1 0 10 14·5%
Poultry	—	—	—	1 10 1 19·5%	1 3 10 15·7%	0 19 8 13·8%
Other stock ...	0 6 4 1·5%	0 2 10 0·7%	0 3 10 1·1%	—	—	—
Live stock and live stock products	12 7 2 59·7%	12 11 0 62·6%	11 6 5 64·5%	7 14 8 100·0%	7 10 8 98·9%	7 3 7 99·9%
Other sources ...	6 3 3 29·8%	5 10 7 27·6%	4 2 5 23·6%	1 19 10 —	1 0 5 —	0 15 10 —
Total	20 13 9	20 0 8	17 10 9	9 14 7	8 12 10	7 19 6

* Danish Report, Table 25, p. 46. † Norwegian Report, Table V, p. 106. ‡ Swedish Report, Table 11, p. 21.
|| Swiss Report, Tables on pp. 60, 61, 62, 63.

On the other hand, the figures in Table B must be used with extreme care in attempting any comparisons of the value of the gross production of one country with another, since such comparisons are necessarily limited, first, by the difficulties resulting from the use of various currencies, and, secondly, by the modification of methods used in computing the gross output itself. The dangers which are always attendant on the first difficulty are increased in the present case by the unstable state of the exchanges during the year of the study, the fluctuations being considerable for both Norway and Denmark. Although there are various minor modifications in the methods of the four European countries, the second limitation applies more particularly to any comparison of the results of the Carmarthenshire study with the results from abroad, since the former are based on financial accounts kept for one year only, while the others are extracted from a scientific system of account keeping extending over several years. So far as the value of the gross production is concerned, the chief influences of this are, first, that the Carmarthenshire figures take no account of the annual appreciation, and, secondly, the value of the produce consumed by the household is given as an estimated total and is not distributed between its various sources[1]. Bearing these reservations in mind, and so far as the table can be accepted as an indication, the holdings of Denmark and Switzerland show the highest value per acre for the gross output, Norway coming third, while the value is least for the Carmarthenshire holdings.

The figures in the table which show the percentage distribution of the gross production between its various sources supply a useful indication of the general nature of the economy of the small holdings, and the chief tendencies can be clearly distinguished.

In the first place the proceeds from crops are seen to be of secondary importance in all the countries. They are highest for Norway and least for Denmark, while they have already been shown to be practically negligible for the Carmarthenshire

[1] In the table this estimate is given in the row "Other sources," there being no other sources of production in the case of Carmarthenshire.

holdings. The sale of crop produce is, however, only partly an indication for the importance of such crops in the system of farming. Thus, in each of these foreign countries about 40 per cent. of the area of the holdings is under arable cultivation, much more cereals, roots, and other fodder crops being raised. In order to show the great difference in this respect from the Welsh holdings, the following figures of the percentage distribution of the land in the Danish group under 25 acres in extent can be taken as a typical example[1].

				%
Cereals	...	...	...	42·2
Roots and potatoes	...		...	21·4
Grass and catch crops			...	32·8
Beet	...	...	...	1·9
Seeds for sale	...	...	...	0·9
Fallow	...	...	...	0·8
				100·0

It is obvious that such figures as these describe holdings whereon an intensive arable system is practised. In the case of the Swiss holdings it should be stated that fruit and vine form an important source of revenue, viz. over 16 per cent. in the first group, over 15 per cent. in the second group, and over 11 per cent. in the third group. In the table these are shown under "Other sources" and, therefore, explain the relatively higher figures in this row for Switzerland.

The source of most of the production of all the small holdings is seen to be from live stock and live stock products, which account for over 86 per cent. in Denmark, over 69 per cent. in Norway, over 71 per cent. in Sweden, and over 59 per cent. in Switzerland, while for the Carmarthenshire holdings practically the whole income is so derived. If it be admitted that live stock and live stock products are more in the nature of luxuries than are cereals and other crop products, then, from the point of view of the production of the necessaries of life, a possible criticism of the activities of small holdings may be indicated in this characteristic of their produce.

Cattle appear to be the sheet anchor of the small holdings

[1] Danish Report, *op. cit.* Table 14, p. 27.

in all the countries, accounting for, approximately, a half of the total production of each of the eighteen groups shown in the table. Further, this importance is seen to depend mostly on the preparation of dairy produce, which makes up the greater part of the income from cattle. Thus dairy produce accounts for over 80 per cent. of the total cattle production of the three Scandinavian countries, and similarly for over 60 per cent. in Switzerland. Inasmuch as in all these countries practically all the milk is sold off the holdings, the comparison in this case must be with the milk-selling holdings of the Carmarthenshire survey where also over 70 per cent. of the total sales from cattle consisted of the sale of milk. Incidentally, it is important to remember that in these four foreign countries the milk industry of the small holdings is organised almost entirely on co-operative lines.

Pigs come next in importance in all the countries, although both the actual pig production per acre as well as the percentage which it forms of the total production are considerably higher for Denmark. The Danish holdings can, indeed, be taken as typical of those depending mainly on the dual sources of dairy cattle and pigs. Here co-operative bacon factories play an important rôle, and these are increasing rapidly in the other countries as well.

Both horses and sheep are seen to be comparatively unimportant throughout. Sheep are entirely absent from the Danish and Swedish holdings, while for Norway and Switzerland the figures in the table include also the production from goats.

So far as the table indicates there seems to be considerable similarity in the production per acre from poultry between the Danish and the Carmarthenshire holdings, while the relative importance of poultry in the total production of the Welsh holdings is considerably higher. Poultry apparently receive less attention in the three other countries. In these countries, as well as in Denmark, increasing importance is attached to the culture of bees; thus, for example, in the second Swiss group nearly 1·5 per cent. of the total production is from this source.

Not only is the total production per acre of the small holding higher than that of the large farm, but the actual surplus for sale is also higher per acre. This has already been shown to be so for the Carmarthenshire holdings, while the evidence from each of the other countries is to the same effect. The Danish figures which are given in detail in the following table may be taken as a typical example[1].

Disposal of gross output per acre on Danish holdings

Acres	Crops		Live stock		All Produce	
	Home consumed	Sold	Home consumed	Sold	Home consumed	Sold
	£ s. d.	£ s. d.	£ s. d.	£ s. d.	£ s. d.	£ s. d.
Under 25	0 12 11 *40·5 %*	0 18 8 *59·5 %*	0 17 10 *3·7 %*	19 16 7 *96·3 %*	2 13 3 *11·3 %*	20 19 5 *88·7 %*
25–50	0 8 9 *36·5 %*	0 15 7 *63·5 %*	0 13 8 *4·4 %*	15 0 6 *95·6 %*	1 16 1 *10·0 %*	16 2 1 *90·0 %*
50–75	0 8 9 *26·0 %*	1 4 9 *74·0 %*	0 9 2 *2·3 %*	13 17 11 *97·7 %*	1 8 11 *8·6 %*	15 4 2 *91·4 %*
75–125	0 7 11 *19·7 %*	1 11 11 *80·3 %.*	0 7 3 *3·0 %*	12 6 9 *97·0 %*	1 5 1 *8·2 %*	13 19 11 *91·8 %*
125–250	0 5 0 *12·9 %*	1 14 3 *87·1 %*	0 7 3 *4·3 %*	9 14 8 *95·7 %*	1 0 2 *8·0 %*	11 10 5 *92·0 %*
Over 250	0 2 4 *3·2 %*	3 13 0 *96·8 %*	0 5 0 *7·3 %*	6 10 9 *92·7 %*	0 13 4 *6·1 %*	10 5 8 *93·9 %*

The amount of the produce per acre consumed by the family is seen to be in inverse ratio to the size of the holding, so also is the percentage which such consumption forms of the total production. Nevertheless, the smallest holdings sell more than double as much as the largest farms, viz. £20. 19*s*. 5*d*. per acre for holdings under 25 acres and £10. 5*s*. 8*d*. per acre for holdings over 250 acres. There is a difference, however, between the disposal of crop products and the disposal of the stock products, since the amount sold per acre of the former increases relatively to the size of the holding.

[1] Danish Report, Table 27, p. 49. For the other countries see as follows: Norwegian Report, Table 26, p. 34; Swedish Report, Table 13, p. 24; and Swiss Report, pp. 76–78.

The smaller farms appear in the same superior position when their production is expressed in calorific values, as the following figures for Switzerland help to illustrate[1].

Production in calories per acre

Acres	Home consumed	Sold	Total
7·5–12·5	415,360	553,720	969,080
12·5–25	271,000	648,880	919,880
25–37·5	207,200	605,800	813,000
37·5–75	178,880	615,360	794,240
Over 75	125,240	555,000	680,240

Thus the total production in calories per acre is seen to decrease with the increase in the size of the holding, while a similar inverse movement also characterises the amount of calories consumed by the household. The close ratio of the amount consumed at home to the amount sold for small holdings under 12·5 acres in extent may be taken as an indication that these are near the lower limit, where production of a surplus for sale becomes of secondary importance to production for consumption by the producers themselves.

3. GROSS EXPENSES

The working expenses of the continental small holdings, which are analysed in this section, are made up of the following constituents. First, all money expenses, with the exception of payments for the increase of any part of the agricultural capital, such as payments for the purchase of live stock, which are not considered to be costs of production since such increase is excluded from the production itself; likewise interest, rent, and personal taxes are also excluded. Secondly, remuneration for the manual work of the occupier and his family, as well as the value of payments in kind to hired labour. And, thirdly, normal depreciation of buildings, cultivations, machinery and horses, together with the value of any reduction in the supplies of stores and materials.

[1] Swiss Report, p. 78.

In the Carmarthenshire survey, on the other hand, it was not possible to follow such a scientific process, since the actual data were limited to the simple financial accounts of one year. Thus, purchases of live and dead stock may, or may not, be regarded as taking the place of depreciation, and rent has been shown to be a considerable item of expense. In order, therefore, to bring these results as near as possible in line with the results of the other countries, the total expenses shown in the last section of Table C have been obtained by deducting rent and interest on capital from the estimate already analysed in Table XXXVI.

It will be realised, from what has just been written, that it is even more difficult to compare the gross expenses of one country with another than it is to compare the gross production. However, so far as the table goes, the same general tendencies can be discerned for the gross expenses. Thus, Denmark and Switzerland show the highest cost per acre, Norway coming third and Sweden fourth. Again, within each country there is a similar inverse movement of the total expense per acre with the increase in the size of the holding.

The table is much more reliable when the various items of expense are under consideration than it is as an indication of the amount of the total expenses, and much can be learnt from it as to the relative importance of such expenses to the smallholder. Thus, in the first place, the wages bill is seen to be both actually and relatively the most considerable item in the expenses of all the holdings in each country. The most important factor here is the ratio of hired labour to family labour, and the method of assessing the remuneration of the latter. This ratio is shown to move directly with the size of the holding in Denmark, Norway, and Switzerland; details are not given separately for Sweden. Although family labour is the predominant item throughout, hired labour is also considerable (even on the smaller holdings) in Denmark and particularly in Norway, a fact which is difficult to explain[1]. The highest total wages bill per acre is shown for Switzerland, Norway and Denmark coming second and third respectively. These

[1] Paul Borgedal, *Driftsresultater fra Jordbruket pa Sorlandet*, 1924, p. 15.

TABLE C. Gross expenses per acre, and percentage distribution of expenses

	Denmark*			Norway†			Sweden‡		
	A	B	C	A	B	C	A	B	C
	£ s. d.	£ s. d.	£ s. d.	£ s. d.	£ s. d.	£ s. d.	£ s. d.	£ s. d.	£ s. d.
Family wages ...	7 8 8 / 36·3%	3 5 9 / 22·3%	2 6 0 / 17·0%	7 2 11 / 42·9%	2 12 4 / 19·2%	1 17 7 / 16·7%	—	—	—
Wages of hired labour	1 8 6 / 6·9%	2 15 6 / 18·8%	3 5 5 / 24·2%	1 16 3 / 10·9%	4 17 3 / 35·5%	4 2 6 / 36·8%	—	—	—
Total wages ...	8 17 2 / 43·2%	6 1 3 / 41·1%	5 11 5 / 41·2%	8 19 2 / 53·8%	7 9 7 / 54·7%	6 0 1 / 53·5%	7 9 10 / 68·6%	4 15 9 / 65·3%	5 5 0 / 47·9%
Feeding Stuffs Bill	7 3 9 / 35·1%	4 15 5 / 32·4%	4 3 8 / 30·9%	2 4 5 / 13·3%	1 19 2 / 14·3%	1 9 10 / 13·3%	0 16 3 / 7·4%	0 10 6 / 6·8%	0 19 1 / 8·5%
Manure Bill ...	0 13 4 / 3·2%	0 13 4 / 4·5%	0 13 4 / 4·9%	0 13 6 / 4·1%	0 16 1 / 5·9%	0 15 5 / 6·9%	0 8 7 / 3·9%	0 5 4 / 3·6%	0 6 3 / 2·8%
Other expenses ...	3 15 10 / 18·5%	3 4 8 / 22·0%	3 2 4 / 23·0%	4 15 8 / 28·8%	3 8 5 / 25·1%	2 19 1 / 26·3%	2 3 11 / 20·1%	1 15 10 / 24·3%	4 9 9 / 40·8%
Total ...	20 10 1	14 14 8	13 10 9	16 12 7	13 13 3	11 4 5	10 18 7	7 7 5	11 0 1

	Switzerland§			Carmarthenshire		
	A	B	C	A	B	C
	£ s. d.	£ s. d.	£ s. d.	£ s. d.	£ s. d.	£ s. d.
Family wages …	— (82%)‖	— (71%)‖	— (50%)‖	5 5 0 *59.3%*	3 18 4 *53.9%*	3 2 6 *48.4%*
Wages of hired labour	— (18%)‖	— (29%)‖	— (50%)‖	0 0 1 *0.0%*	0 0 2 *0.1%*	0 2 1 *1.6%*
Total wages …	12 3 0 *53.2%*	9 19 8 *48.7%*	8 4 5 *44.9%*	5 5 1 *59.3%*	3 18 6 *54.0%*	3 4 7 *50.0%*
Feeding Stuffs Bill	1 15 7 *7.8%*	2 1 2 *10.1%*	1 19 1 *10.7%*	2 2 5 *24.0%*	1 12 6 *22.3%*	1 15 11 *27.8%*
Manure Bill …	0 9 6 *2.1%*	0 8 10 *2.1%*	0 8 1 *2.2%*	0 3 1 *1.8%*	0 2 1 *1.4%*	0 2 8 *2.1%*
Other expenses …	8 9 8 *36.9%*	8 0 6 *39.1%*	7 14 8 *42.2%*	1 6 5 *14.9%*	1 12 5 *22.3%*	1 6 0 *20.1%*
Total … …	22 17 9	20 10 2	18 6 3	8 17 0	7 5 6	6 9 2

* Danish Report, Table 30, p. 56.　† Norwegian Report, Table 19, p. 26.
‡ Swedish Report, Table 15, p. 29.　§ Swiss Report, Tables on pp. 30, 31.
‖ These percentages show the ratio of family to hired labour only.

countries stand in the same relation when arranged according to their relative expense on family and hired labour, and this may be an indication of the possible undue inflation of the total wages bill resulting from the assessment of family labour at current rates of wages. Allowance must also be made for differences in the degree of accuracy exercised in recording the actual labour employment. This is undoubtedly responsible for the lower labour bill per acre of the Carmarthenshire holdings[1]. What the table shows clearly is the general tendency of the total labour bill per acre to fall with the increase in the size of the holding, a tendency which obtains for each country, and which is a natural corollary to the greater intensity of labour on the smaller farms.

The expense incurred in the purchase of feeding stuffs and manures supplies some indication of the nature of the farming. The most interesting feature emphasised by the table is the very much higher amount of feeding stuffs bought in Denmark. This shows the dependence of Danish agriculture on imports, a fact which told adversely on the small holdings in that country during the great war[2]. The percentage which purchases of feeding stuffs form of the total expenses is also considerably higher in Denmark, and it is interesting to note that the second place is occupied by the Carmarthenshire farms. There is a general tendency in all countries for the feeding stuffs bill per acre to be higher for the smaller holdings. On the other hand, the manure bill per acre does not vary much from group to group, it is highest for Norway and lowest for Carmarthenshire.

The chief items included under "Other expenses" are tradesmen's bills, veterinary and other fees, insurance, amortisation and other incidental expenses. Amortisation is the most important in all the foreign countries, being very considerable for both Norway and Switzerland, where the capitalisation per acre is also high as a result of the very extensive outlay on buildings in these two countries.

[1] A charge is also made for wages of management in the case of the continental countries; this naturally decreases with the size of the farm, being practically negligible for the small holdings.

[2] O. H. Larsen, *De Okonomiske Vilkaar for Landbrug af Forskellig Storrelse under og efter Verdenskrigen*, 1924.

4. THE RESULTS OF FARMING

When the figures in Table C are deducted from those in Table B, the results may be considered to represent the net returns per unit of land, and can, therefore, be used as some criterion of the efficiency in the use of this factor of production. Such a conception of net returns can also be regarded as the reward obtained from the capital invested. If it is expressed as a percentage of that capital itself, a similar standard of the efficiency in the use of capital is obtained. Such a method of analysis is applied to the results of all the holdings in the countries under investigation, and these are summarised in the following table, which shows the net returns per acre together with the percentages which such returns form of the capital invested:

TABLE D. Net returns per acre, and as per cent. of agricultural capital

	Denmark*			Norway†		
	A	B	C	A	B	C
	£ s. d.	£ s. d.	£ s. d.	£ s. d.	£ s. d.	£ s. d.
Net returns	3 2 11	3 3 7	3 2 4	1 10 10	0 7 7	0 19 7
Do. as per cent. of agricultural capital	5·3 %	6·1 %	6·3 %	1·2 %	0·8 %	2·0 %

	Sweden‡		Switzerland§		
	A	B	A	B	C
	£ s. d.	£ s. d.	£ s. d.	£ s. d.	£ s. d.
Net returns	1 6 9	1 2 5	2 4 0 (deficit)	0 9 6 (deficit)	0 15 6 (deficit)
Do. as per cent. of agricultural capital	2·8 %	2·8 %	(−) 1·6 %	(−) 0·4 %	(−) 0·7 %

* Danish Report, Table 32, p. 61.
† Norwegian Report, Table 27, p. 35.
‡ Swedish Report, Huvudtabell I, pp. 65, 67.
§ Swiss Report, Tables on p. 82.

The table is not very successful in showing any pronounced tendencies, although it certainly shows the Danish holdings as occupying the most favourable position, while in Switzerland there was in 1922 an adverse balance per acre. In order, therefore, to show more clearly the influence of the size of the holding on the net returns, the Danish and Swiss data will now be analysed more closely. The Norwegian and Swedish results do not lend themselves to this purpose, since they are presented for various parts of the country only.

A. *Denmark*

The chief factors which require to be known in order to arrive at any criterion of the result of the agricultural undertaking are shown in the next table, which gives in a summarised form the results of 534 Danish holdings of all sizes for the year 1922–23.

TABLE E. Results of 534 Danish holdings[1]

Acres	No. of holdings	Gross output per acre	Gross expenses per acre	Net returns per acre	Agricultural capital per acre	Net returns as per cent. of agricultural capital	Balance per acre after allowing for normal interest on capital
		£ s. d.	£ s. d.	£ s. d.	£ s. d.		£ s. d.
Under 25	45	23 13 0	20 10 1	3 2 11	59 11 7	5·3	0 3 10
25–50	88	17 18 3	14 14 8	3 3 7	51 16 11	6·1	0 13 4
50–75	121	16 13 1	13 10 9	3 2 4	49 6 8	6·3	0 14 10
75–125	154	15 4 11	12 19 1	2 5 10	47 18 11	5·8	0 9 11
125–250	74	12 10 7	10 10 0	2 0 7	43 12 7	4·7	minus 0 0 9
Over 250	52	10 19 0	9 2 11	1 16 1	43 2 9	4·2	minus 0 4 7

The inverse ratio of both the gross output and the gross sales to the size of the holding, which has already been observed several times, is seen to become even more pronounced as the holdings increase in extent. A similar tendency in the resultant

[1] Danish Report, Table 34, p. 66, and Table 36, p. 68.

of these two is also shown, and the net returns drop from £3. 2s. 11d. per acre for the small holdings under 25 acres to £1. 16s. 1d. for large farms of 250 acres and above.

For the year 1922–23 this comparatively higher net return on the smaller holdings in Denmark was almost entirely due to the good conditions obtaining for the production of milk and bacon, which together include nearly the whole of the activities of the smaller farmers[1]. Again, an analysis of the variation in the size of the net output within any group reveals the best results as depending, either, on better soil conditions, or, on low working expenses[2]—the two factors which in the case of the Carmarthenshire survey also tended to equalise the results of the highland and lowland holdings.

Generally, however, a high net return per acre is associated with an equally high degree of capitalisation, and in order to show this the amount of agricultural capital invested per acre has also been inserted in the table. When the net returns are expressed as a percentage of the agricultural capital, the resulting figure is called the *forrentingsprocent*, and forms a useful indication of efficiency. It will be seen that there is less variation from group to group in this factor than in the net returns themselves, and this is accounted for by the complementary influence of the capitalisation. There is, however, a greater degree of variation within the small holdings than within the larger farms[3]. For example, 18 per cent. of the small holdings under 25 acres in extent had a *forrentingsprocent* of over 10, while 20 per cent. were under 0; the corresponding figures for the 25–50 acre group were 19 per cent. and 2 per cent. On the other hand, on about 90 per cent. of the holdings in the large farm group this factor lies between 0 and 10. Thus it will be seen that, although the small holdings contain a comparatively high proportion of the more successful results, they also contain a higher proportion of holdings for which unfavourable results were obtained.

Within any one group there seems to be a correlation between a high *forrentingsprocent* and, either, a large stock of pigs, a first-class herd of milch cows, or, a large area under sugar beet.

[1] *Ibid.* p. 62. [2] *Ibid.* p. 64. [3] *Ibid.* p. 64.

The holdings of the poorer soils of West Jutland, on the other hand, show that it is possible to compensate for a low gross output by reducing costs to a minimum. It is also very interesting to read that the characteristic of the majority of the holdings with inferior results is a small gross output, with comparatively high costs particularly in labour; but it is rare to find among the poorer results that of a holding with both a large gross output and high costs, if such costs are primarily due to heavy purchases of feeding stuffs. It might therefore be inferred that the more intensively farmed holdings give the better results.

The surplus per acre after allowing for normal interest on capital[1], which is shown in the last column of the table, can be used as an alternative standard for judging the results of the various size-groups. It shows that the capitalisation of the small holdings is so high that the interest has nearly swallowed the whole of the net returns. The most favourable results obtain for the two groups of holdings between 25 and 75 acres in extent, while the larger farms, in spite of their comparatively lower capitalisation, do not provide a sufficient covering for interest.

When the net surplus which remains after all the expenses, including interest on capital, have been met is added to the calculated remuneration of family labour, the result gives a fairly accurate estimate of what may be termed the "family income," which was as follows for the various size-groups:

			Family income per acre*		
Acres			£	s.	d.
Under 25	...	...	7	12	6
25–50 ...	...	...	3	18	8
50–75 ...	...	...	3	0	10
75–125 ...	...	...	2	7	11
125–250	...	...	1	5	6
Over 250	...	...	0	8	4

[1] Normal interest is calculated thus: 4 per cent. value of land, 5 per cent. value of buildings and cultivations, 6 per cent. value of stock and machinery, and 8 per cent. value of stores, or, roughly 5 per cent. value of total agricultural capital.

* Danish Report, Table 38, p. 72.

The influence of the size of the holding on this factor is very obvious, thus it falls from £7. 12s. 6d. per acre in the smaller holdings to 8s. 4d. per acre on the largest farms. This is due almost entirely to the much greater importance of family labour on the smaller holdings, while on the large farms practically only the management falls to the lot of the occupier.

It is very interesting to note that the income per person on an average small holding of 14½ acres, when calculated in this way, is remarkably similar to the wages of the hired labourer, the actual figures being, approximately, £43 and £44 per annum respectively. But Danish experience for the five year period from 1917 to 1922 has shown, however, that the income of the smallholder is more sensitive than that of the hired man to changes in the value of money[1].

It still remains to examine the remuneration of labour—both family and hired—in terms of the actual number of persons employed. For this purpose the following figures of the acreage of cultivated area per person as well as the remuneration per person are useful[2]:

	Cultivated area per person	Total wages (hired and family) per person		
Acres	Acres	£	s.	d.
Under 25	10·2	36	18	0
25–50	13·1	35	5	0
50–75	12·9	40	4	0
75–125	17·7	40	1	0
125–250	22·5	38	7	0
Over 250	26·0	37	1	0

The second column provides a good illustration of the greater intensity of employment as the holdings decrease in size. Thus, on an average of all the holdings one man is employed per every 17·5 acres approximately, but there is almost twice the number for small holdings under 25 acres, while on the largest farms only one person is engaged per every 26 acres. It is only natural, therefore, to expect the total remuneration per person

[1] *Ibid.* p. 72. [2] *Ibid.* Table on p. 73.

employed to move in the opposite direction. But the figures show that there is very little difference in the wages on the smallest holdings and on the largest farms, and this is probably due to a less efficient management on the latter. Here, again, the best results are shown for the medium-sized holdings where the average annual wage per person is approximately £40.

B. *Switzerland*

The results from Switzerland form a necessary complement to the above, since they show how the same general tendencies as were observed for one year in Denmark also obtain for a considerable period of years. Thus the Swiss results reach back to 1901, and over 6000 annual results are included in the investigation. Moreover, the material from Switzerland was considerably less disorganised during the war period, and, consequently, it provides a safer basis for showing the influence of the time factor on the results of holdings of various sizes. The relevant details are summarised in the following table:

TABLE F. 6057 annual results of Swiss holdings.
From 1901 to 1922[1]

Acres	No. of holdings	Gross output per acre			Gross expenses per acre			Net returns per acre			Agricultural capital per acre			Net returns in per cent. of agricultural capital
		£	*s.*	*d.*	£	*s.*	*d.*	£	*s.*	*d.*	£	*s.*	*d.*	
7·5–12·5	622	19	3	3	15	17	9	3	5	6	115	15	3	2·79
12·5–25	2457	16	5	10	12	1	1	4	4	9	102	7	2	4·14
25–37	1367	14	13	5	10	7	8	4	5	9	92	19	3	4·61
37–75	1247	13	7	8	9	5	10	4	1	10	85	5	7	4·80
Over 75	364	11	8	8	7	18	0	3	10	8	63	3	7	5·59

It provides ample corroboration of the chief tendencies that have been repeatedly observed during the course of this study, viz. the inverse ratios of the capitalisation, gross output, and

---

[1] Swiss Report, Tables on pp. 58, 74, 82. The figures in this table have been converted at the par rate of exchange.

the gross expenses to the size of the holding. It also shows
in the case of the smaller holdings the detrimental effect of
the high expense per acre on the net returns, which form
only 2·79 per cent. of the capital invested on holdings under
12·5 acres, as compared with 5·59 per cent. on holdings over
75 acres in extent.

REFERENCES

DENMARK

Danmarks Statistisk Aarbog. Copenhagen, 1923.

Undersøgelser over Landbrugets Driftsforhold. Parts I–VII.
Copenhagen, 1916–1923.

O. H. LARSEN. *De Okonomiske Vilkaar for Landbrug af
Forskellig Storrelse under og efter Verdenskrigen.* Copenhagen, 1924.

NORWAY

Jordbrukstellingen i Norge, 1 Jan. 1918. *Norges Offisielle
Statistikk.* VII. 12. Oslo, 1921.

*De Faste Eiendommer i arene 1916–1920. Norges Offisielle
Statistikk.* VII. 89. Oslo, 1923.

Regnskapresultater fra Norske Gardsbruk, 1922–23. (Det Kgl.
Selskap for Norges Vel.) Fredrikshald, 1924.

PAUL BORGEDAL. *Driftsresultater fra Jordbruket pa Sorlandet.*
(1924.)

—— *Den Okonomiske Grense for Jordutstykning.* (1922.)

SWEDEN

Arealinventeringen och Husdjursrakningen den 1. *Juni* 1919,
av *Kungl. Statistiska Centralbyran,* II. Stockholm, 1920.

Räkenskapresultat från Svenska Jordbruk, I–IX. Malmö, 1914–
1923.

ERNST HOIJER. *Undersokning av det Storre och Mindre Jord-
brukets Produktion.* Stockholm, 1919.

SWITZERLAND

Ergebnisse der eidg. Betriebszahlung vom 9. Aug. 1905. Band 2. (*Schweizerische Statistik*, 168. Lieferung.) Bern, 1906.

Untersuchungen betreffend die Rentabilität der schweizerischen Landwirtschaft im Erntejahre 1922–23. Bern, 1924.

DR ERNST LAUER. *Der Einfluss der Betriebsgrosse auf dem landwirtschaftlichen Rohertrag.* Jena, 1916.

L. HANNES GEBHARD. *Smabruket i Skandinavien.* Helsingfors. (1923.)

INDEX